two needles, many knits

two needles, many knits

The New Knitter's Guide with Easy Patterns

Quayln Stark

callisto
publishing
an imprint of Sourcebooks

Copyright © 2024 by Callisto Publishing LLC
Cover and internal design © 2024 by Callisto Publishing LLC
Photographs © Elysa Weitala: cover, texture backgrounds, ii, iii, v, vi, ix, x, 2, 15, 16, 17, 68 (background), 72, 73, 74, 75, 76, 78, 80, 82, 84, 86, 89, 90, 93, 94, 95, 96, 98, 101, 102, 105, 106, 109, 110, 111, 112, 115, 116, 121, 122, 126, 132
Author photo courtesy of Emery Stark
Art Director: Lisa Schreiber
Art Producer: Stacey Stambaugh
Production Editors: Ashley Polikoff & Rachel Taenzler
Production Manager: Martin Worthington

Published by Callisto Publishing LLC C/O Sourcebooks LLC
P.O. Box 4410, Naperville, Illinois 60567-4410
(630) 961-3900
callistopublishing.com

Library of Congress Cataloging-in-Publication Data is on file with the publisher.

Printed and bound in China.
OGP 10 9 8 7 6 5 4 3 2 1

*To three
of my biggest supporters:
Polly Reeves, Yolanda Olguin,
and Daniel Stark.*

Contents

Introduction

In your hands, you hold the key to unlocking your newest hobby and passion! As a fiber arts teacher, I'm often asked which medium is my favorite. Just between us, knitting takes the cake. There's something about the rhythm of the stitching and the clicking of the needles that's almost meditative.

That said, I'll be the first to admit that learning to knit may not always feel this way at the start. As someone who is self-taught, I had my fair share of mishaps at the beginning. I have a few too-small beanies and frogged (unraveled and restarted) shawls in my knitting pile. But what I love about knitting is that though mistakes happen, you can always unravel your yarn and start again. Knitting may look like magic, but it becomes intuitive with practice. With knitting, there are only two stitches to learn: the humble knit and purl. After you have those under your belt, every other stitch is just a variation.

In this book, we'll cover everything an absolute beginner needs to have and know to create beautiful, modern knit pieces. We'll start with the basics, such as yarn and needle selection, and work all the way up to cable work and garment construction. Starting a new hobby can be intimidating, but learning to knit will be a breeze with the step-by-step tutorials and practice patterns we'll use to build your foundation skills. Once you're confident in your knitting, we'll work through fifteen patterns that will build your growing knowledge. By the time you finish this book, you'll have every skill and technique you need to knit the handmade world of your dreams! You'll also walk away with fifteen gorgeous pieces that are sure to impress. And nothing beats the joy of receiving a compliment about a project and getting to say the magic words: "Thanks, I knit it myself."

How to Use This Book

This book is designed to help you learn to knit step-by-step. Part 1 explains the knitting process, from the basics of reading a yarn label to casting-on and binding-off. You will learn how to make increases, decreases, and everything else necessary to complete this book's projects. Each new technique will build on previously learned skills so that you won't feel you've missed a step. Part 2 contains patterns broken out into three levels of difficulty. The patterns in each sequential level increase the skills in your repertoire, so I would recommend working at least one pattern from each level.

Now that we've gone over how the book is organized, we're ready to start.

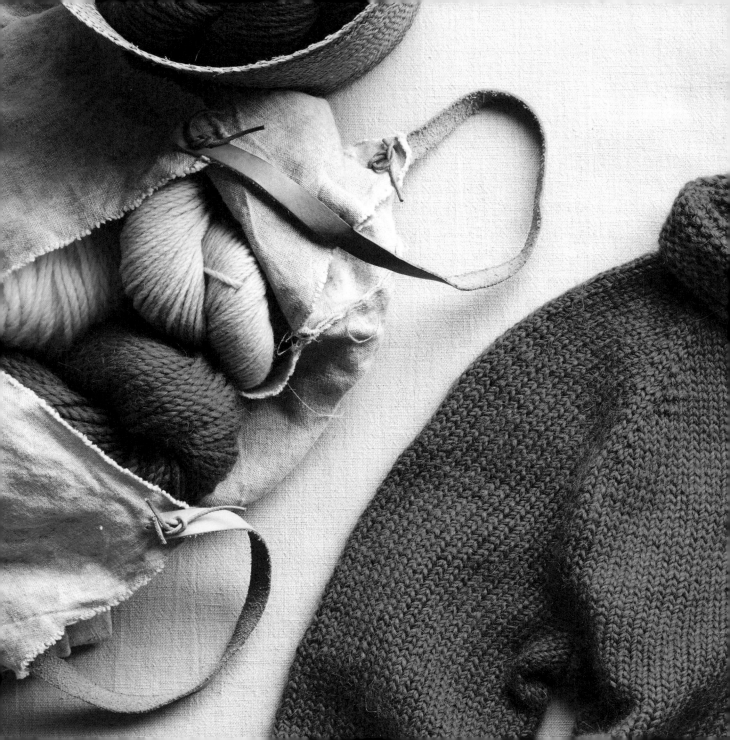

PART 1

Beginner Basics

Before you can make your first knit stitch, there are some things to take into consideration: First, you should get familiar with your tools and supplies. Thankfully, there aren't many. In this section, we'll go over everything you need, from the essentials (just yarn and needles) to other helpful tools. Second, you'll learn how to read a pattern. Here we'll walk through that skill, taking it step-by-step, so that you'll be able to work through a written pattern in no time. We'll also cover other helpful information, like how to properly care for your knits.

TOOLS AND SUPPLIES

What do you need to start knitting? Knitting can be a budget-friendly hobby. There are only a few must-have essentials, and these can be found at any price point. Really, you could start with only needles and yarn. But as with most crafts, there is a handful of supplies that will help you and make creating your projects easier. As you grow in your craft, you'll find that investing in these supplies is worth it in the long run. Let's go over a list of the essentials and then look at beneficial extras you can include in your knitting toolbox.

NEEDLES

When you're starting out as a new knitter, figuring out which needles you should buy for your projects can be confusing.

First, there are the different materials you can choose from: Needles come in wood (like bamboo), plastic, and metal. Wood needles are best for a beginner because they hold on to stitches well, which means you'll end up with fewer dropped stitches. Plastic and metal needles are smoother and better suited for more experienced knitters. Plastic and metal needles cost about the same, but metal is more durable, and performs better in general.

Then there's the question of needle size. Needle size is annotated in both US and metric measurements. Usually, the first number on the package is the US size. For example, one standard knitting needle size is US 7 (4.5 mm). The smaller the number, the thinner the needle. For example, a US 3 (3.25 mm) will be much thinner than a US 9 (5.5 mm). The length of the needles isn't as crucial. All needle sizes come in a wide range of lengths; most knitters will typically start with 7 to 9 inches. As you knit, you will gravitate to your favorite lengths based on personal comfort and the width of your project. Every pattern will have the needle size and type you require, so if you intend to work on a specific project, grab the correct needles. For instance, the first two practice patterns in Level 1 Patterns use US size 8 single-pointed needles. In general, when choosing which size needles to buy, think about what type of projects you expect to make, and the yarns they are made with. Are you planning on knitting baby accessories with thin yarns? If so, you'll want smaller needles, like a US size 4 to 7. If you intend to make projects with chunkier yarns, you may need a US size 9 to 13+.

Of course, size and material aren't the only things you need to consider. You'll also have to know what style of needle you need.

SINGLE-POINTED NEEDLES

Single-pointed needles (also called straight needles) are the classic knitting needle. They come in pairs and can be purchased in a range of lengths. These needles are only used for projects that are knit flat, or seamed. Single-pointed needles are great for things like scarves and shawls.

DOUBLE-POINTED NEEDLES

Double-pointed needles (DPNs for short) are just what they sound like, and have points on both ends. These needles come in groups of five and are shorter in length. DPNs are almost always used for knitting in the round on smaller projects like socks and hats.

CIRCULAR NEEDLES

Circular needles (circs for short) are the most versatile tool in a knitter's collection. With circular needles, you can knit flat or in the round. Circular needles also come in interchangeable sets, which include different-size needle tips and cable lengths that you can swap in and out while knitting. Once you're familiar with working on circular needles, I recommend investing in a good interchangeable set.

Many beginner knitters find that they prefer circs to DPNs, which can be a bit fussy. However, I recommend trying to knit in the round with both circs and DPNs at least once to see which one you prefer.

YARN

Among all the colors, brands, weights, and materials, there are thousands of yarns out there to choose from. How can you know what the best choice is for your project? Each yarn has specific attributes that set it apart and make it ideal for one kind of project or another. Once you know what characteristics you're looking for, you can choose the perfect yarns for your projects.

YARN MATERIALS AND PLIES

When selecting a new yarn, the first things you should look for (besides a cute color) are the materials, ply, and weight. Let's first focus on the material and ply.

Nowadays, yarn can be made of almost anything, so it's important to match your project with suitable fiber content. There are five fiber types that you'll encounter most often: acrylic, wool, plant-based (like cotton or linen), alpaca, and silk. Yarn can be made entirely of a single fiber type or multiple types blended together. If the yarn is a blend, it will have the most characteristics in common with its main component. (There are also novelty yarns, like faux fur or bouclé, which should be considered on a case-by-case basis.)

Most yarn is spun in plies. A ply is a single strand of yarn that is spun directly from fiber. A strong yarn will have two or more plies spun together. (A single-ply yarn will be more likely to split or break when you're knitting and is more likely to pill after slight wear. Because of this, I'd recommend steering clear of single-ply yarn when learning to knit.) When you start selecting yarn for your projects, refer to the following table for help choosing the perfect skein.

YARN TYPE	BEST FOR	WORST FOR
ACRYLIC	Everyday items that need to be laundered regularly. Children's toys that need to stand up to rough treatment.	Warm-weather garments. Colorwork projects.
WOOL	Cold-weather projects. Strong stitch definition. Cable or colorwork projects.	Warm-weather garments. Projects for people with skin sensitivities.
PLANT-BASED	Warm-weather projects. Items that are used often.	Fitted garments or accessories.
ALPACA AND SILK	Items that need to drape.	Fitted garments or accessories.
NOVELTY	Accents for projects made with other yarns.	Projects that are laundered regularly.
SINGLE-PLY	Intentionally felted items.	Items that are used often or laundered regularly.
MULTI-PLY	Most every project.	Intentionally felted items.

YARN WEIGHTS

A yarn's weight is just as important as its fiber content. There are two common ways that yarn weight is referred to: its category distinction and its common name. A category distinction is a numerical value that ranges from 0, which is the thinnest, to 7, which is the thickest. The common name of a yarn's weight is what you will hear referred to most often, and it ranges from lace (the thinnest) to jumbo (the thickest). Check out the following chart for the names and their corresponding categories. The recommended needle sizes are also included. That said, although most yarns come with a recommended needle size listed right on the band (see page 7), some knit patterns may use a larger or smaller needle than the one listed to create different fabric textures. For instance, using a smaller-than-recommended needle size will produce a heavy and dense fabric, whereas using a larger-than-recommended needle size will produce an airy and loose fabric.

YARN CATEGORY	COMMON NAME	RECOMMENDED NEEDLES
0	Lace	US 000 (1.5 mm)–US 1 (2.25 mm)
1	Fingering	US 1 (2.25 mm)–US 3 (3.25 mm)
2	Sport	US 3 (3.25 mm)–US 5 (3.75 mm)
3	DK	US 5 (3.75 mm)–US 7 (4.5 mm)
4	Worsted	US 7 (4.5 mm)–US 9 (5.5 mm)
5	Chunky	US 9 (5.5 mm)–US 11 (8.0 mm)
6	Super Bulky	US 11 (8.0 mm)–US 17 (12.75 mm)
7	Jumbo	US 17 (12.75 mm) and up

WHAT'S ON THE LABEL

Labels are the best way to understand the specifics of your yarn. Most labels will have the following:

A **Brand and line name:** The exact yarn you are working with.

B **Color name/ number:** Needed if additional yarn is required.

C **Yardage and weight:** Critical in knowing how many skeins are needed when substituting yarn. Weight here refers to grams and ounces.

D **Yarn category number:** A yarn icon with the category number inside. If this number is missing, the common name of the yarn should be written.

E **Fiber content:** Percentages of each fiber in your yarn.

F **Auxiliary info:** Country of origin, care instructions, and standard gauge.

GETTING TO KNOW YOUR YARN

Knitting is a tactile experience. You will be touching your yarn and project for hours at a time, so you should take a moment to get to know the yarns you work with.

Wind it up. There are a handful of ways that yarn may be "put up" or packaged. The most traditional is a skein, which looks like a wound cylinder of yarn. Similarly, cakes are shorter, flatter cylinders and are wound in the same way. Yarn can also be hand-wound into a ball, which looks exactly like it sounds. Skeins, balls, and cakes are convenient because they allow you to start knitting immediately without requiring you to prepare your yarn. Finally, there are hanks. This yarn is wound into a large circle (with many layers of yarn going around and around the circle), then twisted in on itself. Before working with a hank, you must unhank it by winding it into a ball or cake first. This can be done by hand or with the help of a yarn swift and yarn winder. See Other Essentials and Useful Tools (right) for more information on these supplies.

Talk to the pros. If there is a local yarn shop near you, reach out. The staff at these shops is there to help you with all your knitting and yarn needs. If you don't have access to a yarn shop, forums and fiber artists online also offer a wealth of information.

OTHER ESSENTIALS AND USEFUL TOOLS

Though you only need yarn and needles to start knitting, there are a few supplies that make life as a knitter easier. All these products have budget-friendly versions, so shop around. These items are listed by level of importance, so try to grab the top ones first.

SCISSORS: Whether you're changing colors or cutting ends, a good pair of small, sharp scissors comes in handy.

YARN NEEDLE (also called a darning or tapestry needle)**:** Needles are used for finishing projects. They help you seam the sides of a project together and weave in loose ends. Look for blunt needles with large eyes.

GAUGE RULER: You'll use this to measure your gauge (though you can also use a regular ruler).

CROCHET HOOK: A small crochet hook is perfect for picking up dropped stitches and fixing mistakes. If you buy only one, a size H (5.0 mm) will be most useful.

STITCH MARKERS: These little plastic or metal loops are used to keep track of rows, increase or decrease points, and pattern repeats.

ROW COUNTER: These are small trackers with numbered dials that are helpful for large-scale projects where row counts are important.

YARN SWIFT AND WINDER: These tools are used to unhank a yarn and turn it into an easy-to-work-with cake.

PROJECT BAG: Most knitters have a dedicated bag to keep their projects in when they're not working on them. There are specially made project bags, but any bag can work.

CARE AND WASHING

Everyone has heard the horror stories of hand-knit sweaters shrinking to half their size in washers. But fear not. Laundering knits isn't as hard as you'd think. When a project needs to be washed, the most important thing to consider is its fiber content. Refer to the laundering instructions on the yarn's ball band when it's available, and keep a record of the information to refer to later. Cotton, wool labeled "superwash," and yarns with 50 percent or more acrylic content will be fine to run through your normal laundering machines on the delicate cycle with cold water. For everything else, I recommend spot washing or handwashing your project with a delicate fabric detergent like Soak or Eucalan, then laying it flat to air-dry. Most people who receive knits as a gift won't do this, so it's best to make their projects in yarn that is machine washable. (This is especially true for items that need to be laundered often, like baby clothes or socks.)

HOW TO READ A PATTERN

For beginning knitters, one of the most intimidating parts of picking up the craft is learning to read patterns. At a glance, patterns look tricky and confusing. Learning to read knitting patterns can seem as hard as learning to read a foreign language. The good news is that you won't be intimidated for long. Knitting patterns are easily understood once you know a few essential terms. And although pattern styles may differ from designer to designer, there'll be common elements.

Let's start with a pattern's introductory information. Every pattern has setup information you need to look at before starting your project. First is a list of the supplies you'll need, including the needles, tools, and yarns. These detailed lists will tell you which size needle you need, and the weight and amount of yarn needed. Finished measurements are also given.

That said, starting a knitting project isn't as simple as just buying the needles and yarn listed in the pattern. To achieve the measurements listed on the pattern, the stitches you create must be close to the size of the original project:

Otherwise, your piece may be larger or smaller than intended. This will also be written in the setup information and is discussed further in the Gauge section for each pattern. (See Gauge, page 36, to learn how to make a swatch to measure your gauge.)

Then the pattern will usually list any special stitches or stitch patterns that are found in the project, and any notes about the pattern that you should keep in mind before starting.

Once you're done reading this introductory material, you'll move on to the pattern's step-by-step instructions. In general, it's best to look at the way knitting patterns are written as a kind of shorthand. Most of what you see in a pattern is a series of abbreviations. Don't let these abbreviations scare you. They're usually straightforward. For instance, the most common abbreviations are "k" for "knit" and "p" for "purl." Most patterns will even include a glossary of the abbreviations you need to know. Any abbreviation not listed in the glossary will be included in the special stitches section, so you will always know what every shortened instruction stands for.

Here's what a simple row could look like in practice:

Row 3: K1, p3, k2, p6.

In plain text, this would translate to:

Row 3: Knit 1 stitch, purl 3 stitches, knit 2 stitches, purl 6 stitches.

See how simple that is?

You'll also see some special characters in the instructions. These include parentheses ( ), brackets [ ], and asterisks*. Parentheses are most often used to add information before or after a row. They will tell you, for instance, if the row is the right or wrong side of the work, different sizing options within a pattern, or how many stitches you should have on your needles after a row. Brackets are used within a row's directions to mark repeating instructions. This means the instructions within brackets are to be repeated a set number of times. The same is true of an asterisk paired with parentheses: When you see an asterisk and parentheses together, all the information within the asterisks will be repeated. Usually, you'll see this when there is a section of a pattern with multiple brackets that needs to be repeated

altogether. Let's work through a couple examples of this together.

Row 2: K3, [p2, k2] *three times*, p2, k3.

In plain text, this would translate to:

Knit 3 stitches; purl 2 stitches and knit 2 stitches, repeating three times total; purl 2 stitches; knit 3 stitches.

Row 2: K3, * (p3, k3) *repeat from * to end of row*.

In plain text, this would translate to:

Knit 3 stitches; purl 3 stitches and knit 3 stitches, repeating until the end of the row.

See what a difference abbreviations and special characters make?

And that's all there is to pattern reading. Once you work through your first few patterns, most of the abbreviations and special characters will be committed to memory, and you'll be able to read through the instructions without checking your glossary.

TERMS

There are some terms you might see in a knitting pattern that have to do with the project as a whole, rather than with the stitches you create. Let's look at some of these terms and break down their meaning.

Tail end vs. working end: When you begin a project, there are two ends of your yarn to be aware of. The tail end of your yarn is the excess yarn left after casting on (the part that hangs down at the end). This yarn will never be used again while you are working your project and should be cut at around 3 to 4 inches for weaving in later. The working end of your yarn is the yarn being pulled from your skein; this is the piece that you are actively knitting with.

Row vs. round: Rows and rounds refer to each completed line of a stitch pattern. These lines are called rows if you're doing flat knitting (going back and forth), and rounds (or "rnds") if you're knitting in the round.

Right vs. wrong side: Most flat patterns that are not reversible will list which side of the work is the "right side" (often shortened to RS) and which is the "wrong side" (often shortened to WS). This is so knitters know which side of the work is meant to face out. This is important when you're working seamed

Right Side

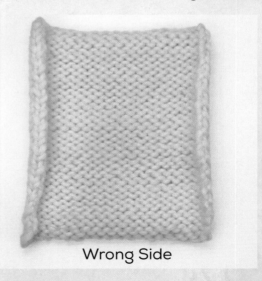

Wrong Side

projects, like garments. The RS or WS will be listed at the beginning of a row, before the actual stitch instructions are given. For example, Row 2 (RS): K3, p3, k3. If you are working on something with a simple stitch pattern, like stockinette stitch, you can easily tell visually which side is which. The right side of the fabric will have the "knit" side of your stitches visible and will resemble many small V's stacked atop one another. The wrong side will have "purl bumps," which resemble U and N shapes stacked off-center from one another. If you still can't tell the right or wrong side apart, then the pattern is likely meant to be reversible.

COUNTING STITCHES AND ROWS

You can count the live stitches on your needle after a completed row, or count the stitches that have already been knit into the fabric. It's important to compare how many stitches are on your needles to the listed stitch counts in a pattern as you work. This is critical when working increase or decrease rows. To do so,

simply count each loop on your needle. Each loop on your needle counts as a stitch. When counting stitches and rows that have already been knit—like when you're checking for gauge—you need to know what to look for. In stockinette, each V counts as one stitch, and the number of V's stacked atop one another is the number of rows or rounds. In garter, rows will look more like U's and N's stacked atop one another, similar to the look of the purl side of stockinette. In this case, each U counts as one stitch, and every set of U/N stacks counts as two rows.

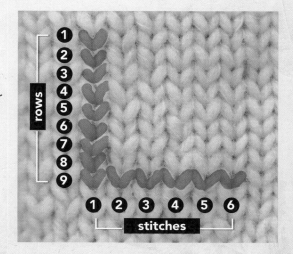

ENGLISH VS. CONTINENTAL

There are two main ways that knitters hold their yarn as they're working. These methods aren't correlated to which hand is dominant but to what feels most comfortable for them (and, usually, how they were taught to knit).

English knitting involves holding your yarn in the hand that holds your working needle (i.e., the needle not holding the last row's stitches). For most knitters, this would be the right hand. This style of knitting involves "throwing" the yarn, meaning that after you insert your needle into a stitch, you wrap the yarn around the needle manually with the front finger of your right hand.

Continental knitting involves holding the yarn in the opposite hand (usually the left), along with the needle holding live stitches from the previous row. In this style, knitters "pick" the yarn, meaning that after you insert your needle into a stitch, the needle catches the working strand of yarn from your finger and pulls it through the stitch. This involves less movement and is commonly believed to be faster and easier on the hands. This is also the easier method for a crocheter, as the yarn position is the same.

Both of these styles are popular. In the next section, I'll show you how to do each. See how they feel and pick the one that works best for you.

Learn to Knit in No Time

In this section, you'll learn all the fundamentals of knitting. We'll go over each of the techniques and stitches in detail, and you'll see just how easy knitting can be. We will start with the cast-on and bind-off, then move on to mastering the knit and purl stitches. After working through all these foundational instructions, you will have every skill required to knit all the patterns in this book—and thousands more.

GETTING STARTED

Before you work on the body of your project, it's important that you know how to begin (how to "cast on" stitches) and how to end (how to "bind off"). There are a few different ways to do both of these things, and you will likely come across many of them during your knitting journey. Here I'm going to demonstrate the two most common methods for casting on and the most common method for binding off. These can be used for almost any project.

SLIP KNOT

A slip knot is the beginning knot and loop of yarn that you make before you cast on. This will always be considered the first stitch of your cast-on.

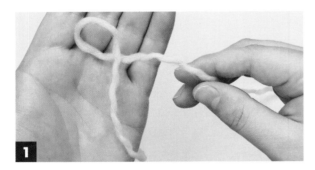

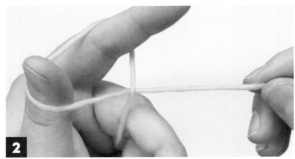

1. Twist your yarn to the left into a small loop (photo 1).

2. Pass your index finger and thumb through the loop from the back (photo 2).

3. Pinch a small length of the tail end of yarn between your two fingers and pull it through the loop. This will create a slip knot.

4. Tighten the working end of yarn to secure the knot, then tighten the tail end of yarn to adjust the size of the slip knot.

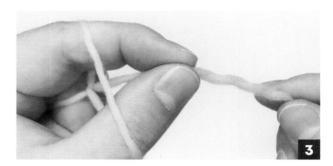

LONG-TAIL CAST-ON

This is the most common cast-on method. As the name suggests, this method uses a long tail of yarn. I suggest pulling out more than you think you need, then cutting the tail later. Though this cast-on method seems like it has many steps, it's actually very simple and quick to do once you learn it.

1. Pull a length of yarn from your working yarn that is about three times longer than the intended width of your finished piece. Make a slip knot at that spot. Place the slip knot on a knitting needle, with the tail end of yarn (the part not attached to the ball) closest to you.

2. Place your index finger and thumb between the working end and the tail end of yarn, and hold both bottoms of those strands together with your other fingers.

3. Point your thumb and index finger up, and bring your knitting needle down, so that it's pointing at the heel of your thumb.

4. Pass the needle under the strand of yarn closest to you on your thumb.

5. Keeping the needle inside the first loop (the one on your thumb), bring the needle over (above) and around the strand of yarn on the far side of your index finger.

6. Using your needle, pull the loop from your index finger back through the loop on your thumb (basically, taking the needle back the way it came).

7. Let go of your thumb loop, letting both your thumb and index finger curl in, and pull the strand to lightly tighten the loop against the needle.

8. Repeat steps 2 to 7 until you have as many stitches on your needle as are required. When you're done, cut the tail to 4 to 5 inches long.

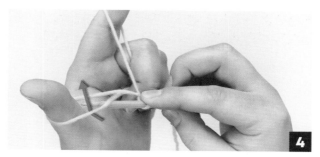

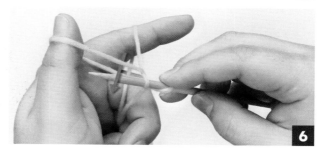

SHORT-TAIL CAST-ON (OR WRAP CAST-ON, BACKWARD-LOOP CAST-ON)

This cast-on can be used instead of a long-tail cast-on at the start of projects, but it's most useful when you need to cast on additional stitches during a project, like when you're knitting the handle of a bag or separating sleeves for a sweater.

1. Make a slip knot in your working yarn, leaving a 4- to 5-inch tail. Place the slip knot on the needle with the tail end of the yarn closest to you.

2. With your working yarn, make a loop that twists to the left.

3. Pass the needle through the back of the loop. Lightly tighten the loop against the needle.

4. Repeat steps 2 and 3 until you have as many stitches on your needle as are required.

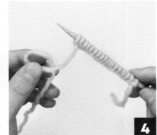

BIND-OFF (ALSO CALLED CAST-OFF)

There are also many ways to bind off or "cast off." This is the most basic and universal method and is suitable for most projects.

1. Knit two stitches.

2. With the needle holding the stitches from the previous row (the one in your left hand), insert the tip of the needle into the first stitch you knit (the one farthest to the right).

3. Pull that first stitch over the second stitch and off your working needle, leaving only the second stitch you worked.

4. Knit one more stitch. Repeat steps 2 to 4 until you have only one loop on your right-hand needle (and none on your left). Clip your working yarn to 4 to 5 inches and pull it through.

THE KNIT STITCH

This stitch is the foundation from which every other stitch is derived. Though it may sound silly, this simple children's rhyme has helped thousands learn the knit stitch: "In through the front door, go around the back, out through the window, and off jumps Jack." Those keywords (in, around, through, and out) describe the process of knitting a stitch perfectly. Let's go over how to do it in both English and Continental styles.

ENGLISH

In this style, you move the yarn with the hand holding the working needle:

1. Hold the needle with your cast-on stitches in your left hand. Hold your working needle (the one without any stitches on it) and the working yarn together in your other hand and loosely wrap the working yarn around your index finger. Identify the next stitch in the row.

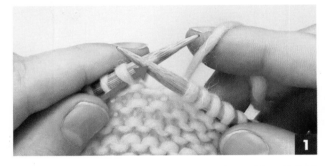

2. Insert the tip of your working needle into the middle of the first stitch on your left-hand needle, from the front to the back so that it ends up behind the other needle.

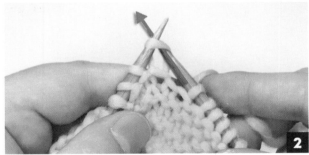

3. With your index finger, wrap the working yarn to the left around the tip of your working needle, from the back of the needle to the front.

4. Pull the wrap of working yarn back through the left-hand stitch, taking the needle out the same way you put it in.

5. After the new stitch is pulled through, slip the old stitch off your other needle.

6. Repeat steps 2 to 5 until the end of the row.

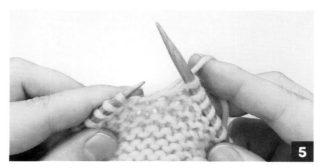

CONTINENTAL

In this style, you move the yarn with the hand holding the nonworking needle:

1. Hold your working needle (the one without any stitches on it) in your right hand. Hold the needle with your cast-on stitches and the working yarn together in your other hand. Loosely wrap the working yarn around your index finger. Identify the next stitch in the row.

2. Insert the tip of your working needle from the front to the back into the middle of the first stitch on your left-hand needle, so that it slides in through the loop of the stitch and ends up behind the other knitting needle.

3. With your index finger, wrap the working yarn to the left around the tip of your working needle, from the back of the needle to the front.

4. Pull the wrap of working yarn back through the left-hand stitch, taking the needle out the same way you put it in.

5. After the new stitch is pulled through, slip the old stitch off your other needle.

6. Repeat steps 2 to 5 until the end of the row.

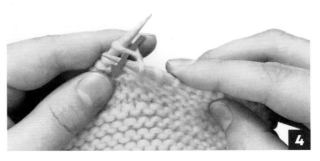

EASY COLOR CHANGES

As a lover of color, I am always looking for different ways to brighten up a project. Thankfully, there are a few beginner-friendly ways of doing just that. If you wish to add a second color of yarn to your project (like when striping or color blocking), the best way is to finish a row or round in one color, cut your working yarn to 4 to 5 inches, then start knitting the next row or round in a new color, leaving a tail of equal length. You can tie the tails into a simple square knot after the first completed line. Afterward, you can weave in the ends. (This is discussed further on page 57.) Alternatively, there are some amazing yarns out there that do the work for you. Some color-changing yarns include an ombre, where the color change is gradual and each shade fades into the next. Others are meant for color blocking and have distinct, abrupt color changes in a single skein. Lastly, there are variegated or self-striping yarns that are like color-blocked yarns with shorter color changes.

THE PURL STITCH

It's best to think of the purl stitch as the exact opposite of the knit stitch. All you need to do is go in the opposite side of the stitch and wrap your yarn in the opposite direction. To do this, you will have to flip how you hold your yarn and where you insert your working needle. However, beyond these small differences, the principles behind the two are the same.

ENGLISH

1. Hold the needle with your live stitches in your left hand. Hold your working needle (the one without any stitches on it) and the working yarn together in your other hand and loosely wrap the working yarn around your index finger at the front of the work. Identify the next stitch in the row.

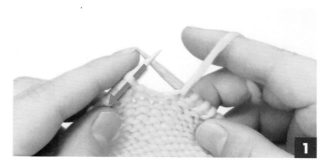

2. Insert the tip of your working needle, going from back to front, into the middle of the first stitch on your left-hand needle, so that it slides in through the loop of the stitch and ends up in front of the other knitting needle.

continued > > >

3. With your index finger, wrap the working yarn to the left around the tip of your working needle, from the back of the needle to the front.

4. Pull the wrap of working yarn back through the left-hand stitch, taking the needle out the same way you put it in.

5. After the new stitch is pulled through, slip the old stitch off your other needle.

6. Repeat steps 2 to 5 until the end of the row.

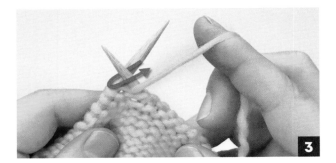

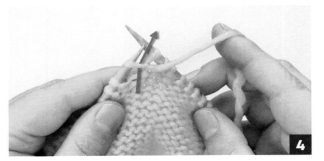

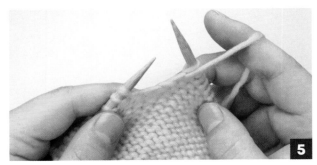

CONTINENTAL

1. Hold your working needle (the one without any stitches on it) in your right hand. Hold the needle with your live cast-on stitches and the working yarn together in your other hand. Loosely wrap the working yarn around your index finger, with the working yarn looping from the front of your finger around to the back of your finger, holding it to the front of the work.

2. Insert the tip of your working needle from the back to the front into the middle of the first stitch on your left-hand needle, so that it slides in through the loop of the stitch and ends up in front of the other knitting needle.

3. With your index finger, wrap the working yarn to the left around the tip of your working needle, from the back of the needle to the front.

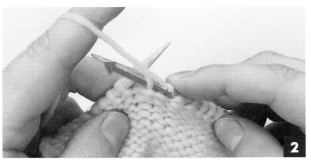

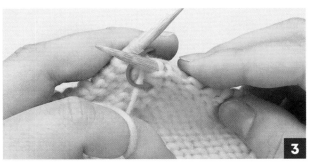

continued > > >

4. Pull the wrap of working yarn back through the left-hand stitch, taking the needle out the same way you put it in.

5. After the new stitch is pulled through, slip the old stitch off your other needle.

6. Repeat steps 2 to 5 until the end of the row.

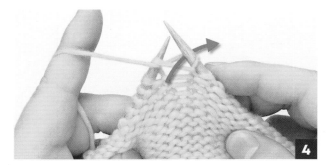

COMBINING STITCHES

Once you've learned to both knit and purl, you can mix the two to create a variety of stunning textures. There are thousands of possible combinations, but there are four main stitch patterns that make up the bulk of knit fabrics and patterns. The first is the garter stitch. In flat knitting, this is working only knit stitches, regardless of the side of the fabric you are working on. This stitch is good for square or rectangular projects that should remain flat and reversible, like blankets or washcloths.

Here are three other easily memorized stitch patterns you should take the time to learn as well.

STOCKINETTE STITCH

The stockinette stitch produces the classic "knit" fabric look. This is the fabric that makes up the body of sweaters, hats, socks, and the like. When knitting flat, it's made by alternating rows of all knits and all purls. To knit flat stockinette:

1. Cast on and begin by knitting one row of only knit stitches; turn your work.

2. For the next row, do only purl stitches; turn your work.

3. Repeat alternating rows of knitting and purling until you have reached the desired length of fabric.

RIB STITCH

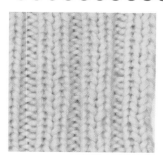

The main characteristic of this fabric is its stretchy structure. Because of its stretch, the rib stitch is perfect for making a cuff or band, like sleeve and sock cuffs or neck- and waist-bands. The key to this stitch is to alternate knit and purl stitches (a few knit followed by a few purl), and then repeat the pattern. You can also choose to have wider or thinner ribs. To work a rib stitch with just two stitches per rib:

1. Cast on an even number of stitches. Knit two stitches, then bring your yarn to the front of your work and purl two stitches. Bring your yarn to the back of the work to knit the next two stitches. Continue to the end of the row; turn your work.

continued > > >

2. On the back of the work, work the opposite stitch into each stitch across. This means if you knit into a stitch on the first row, you will now purl into it, and vice versa. So if you ended the previous row with two knits, you'll start the new row with two purls. If you see a "V" facing you, it means you will knit into it. If you see a "U," then you will purl into it.

3. Repeat steps 1 and 2 until you have reached the desired length of fabric.

Remember, knits and purls are opposites, so to keep your fabric consistent, you will need to reverse each stitch when working on the back of your flat piece.

SEED STITCH

This beautiful stitch pattern is best used to add textural interest to a piece. This stitch pattern is fully reversible and can be used in place of the garter or stockinette stitch for things like blankets or sweaters. You can think of it as blending the rib and garter stitch to create a unique and stunning fabric. To make it, you alternate knit and purl stitches, but in each row, you put knit stitches above purl stitches, and vice versa. To knit a traditional seed stitch:

1. Cast on the desired number of stitches (it's easiest if this is an odd number of stitches). Knit one stitch, then move the yarn to the front of your work; purl one stitch, then move your yarn to the back of the work. Continue this pattern (k1, p1) all the way to the end of the row.

2. On the next row, you will work the exact same stitch pattern as the first row (k1, p1, k1, p1 . . .). Because you had an odd number of stitches, this means you will knit into each knit of the previous row (the stitches that now look like U's), and purl into each purl (the stitches that now look like V's). This means if you ended the previous row with a knit stitch, you will start the next row with a knit stitch.

3. Repeat step 2 until you have reached the desired length of fabric.

PURLS AND CURLS

You may notice that a piece of knitting worked in only stockinette curls in on itself when it's flat (especially along the edges). This is because of the structure of the stitches themselves. From the side, a knit stitch is shaped like a capital C. In a garter stitch, this works to its advantage as the shapes of each row interlock and the yarn pulls first one way and then the other. In stockinette, these rows are stacked atop each other, with all the short sides of the C facing one way, so they roll up on themselves. You can avoid this problem by blocking the piece (see page 58), or by giving the piece a garter border by working 3 to 5 stitches of garter stitch at the beginning and end of each row. Flat stockinette is also good for pieces that will be seamed together, as once a piece is seamed into a shape—like a hat or sweater—the edges can't roll.

TECHNIQUES

As a knitter, you will pick up many techniques along the way. Some are more crucial to the beginning of your knitting journey than others. You'll find that a mix of the following techniques will pop up in patterns more often than not. Because of this, it is best to understand them now, so you can work through a project without stopping every few rows to learn a new skill.

GAUGE

Many knitters consider swatching for gauge annoying, but it is truly necessary. (Personally, I love it; after accumulating a batch of swatches, you can stitch them together to make anything from a blanket to a sweater.) The term "gauge" means the exact length and width of stitches in a specific pattern. For projects that don't need to measure a specific size, you don't need to take gauge into account. For instance, it's perfectly fine if your baby blanket or scarf is a few inches longer or shorter than the given measurements for a pattern. On the other hand, a few inches can make a big difference when you're knitting a hat or sweater. (You wouldn't want to work hours on a cardigan only for it to be two sizes too small.) This is where gauge comes in. The stitch and row/round gauge (the number of stitches and rows that fit into a 4-inch square) will be listed in the information at the beginning of each pattern. You can check your gauge by knitting a gauge swatch as follows.

1. Look over the pattern and sample photo to see what the main stitch pattern for your project is. This will be the stitch pattern you knit to check gauge. (If most of your piece is in stockinette, you'll knit your swatch in stockinette, for example.) Starting with the needle size suggested in the pattern, use the yarn you will make the piece with to cast on about 5 inches of stitches. Knit in the appropriate stitch pattern until your fabric is about 5 inches long. Bind off and block your fabric in the same manner described at the end of the pattern. (For more info on this process, see Blocking, page 58.)

2. After your fabric is blocked, use a ruler to count out how many stitches and how many rows are found within 4 inches of fabric. Compare this to the pattern gauge. If the gauge is off by just one row or stitch, it's not a big deal; you can just block your finished project to the appropriate dimensions. However, if your gauge is off by multiple stitches or rows, you should change needle sizes. If you have more stitches or rows than the pattern gauge says you should, try a larger needle. If you have fewer, try a smaller needle. Make a new swatch with the new needles, and measure again. Repeat this process until you are close to the correct gauge.

KNITTING TWO YARNS TOGETHER

One of the simplest ways to add a bit of flair and visual interest to your knit projects is by knitting two yarns together. You can add a fluffy, complementary strand of lace mohair to a regular yarn to give the project a fuzzy halo, or knit with two yarns of different colors at the same time to get a marled (or "mottled") fabric. Ribbing and seed stitches complement the marled look of holding two yarns together. It's easy. As you cast on and knit your project, hold your two yarns together, and knit with them as if they were just one strand of yarn. You can do this by holding yarn from two separate skeins together in your hand or rolling both strands into a single ball of yarn beforehand.

INCREASES

There are multiple ways to increase the number of stitches in a project, and each offers a different look to the finished fabric. Some are very noticeable, whereas others are less visible. Two of the most common methods, make 1 right and make 1 left, are also two of the most seamless. They differ slightly in how they're made, and once they're finished, they slant in opposite directions.

MAKE 1 RIGHT (M1R)

This increase will show up as a slight slant to the right.

1. Knit up to your increase point. Identify the strand of yarn between the last stitch you knit and the next stitch.

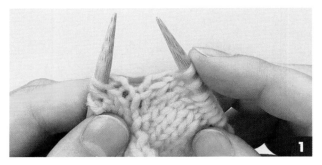

2. Insert the working needle under the strand of yarn between your last knit stitch and the next stitch, putting it in from the front of your work to the back.

3. Pick up the strand with the working needle and place it on the other needle with the leftmost (forward) leg of the strand on the side of the needle facing you.

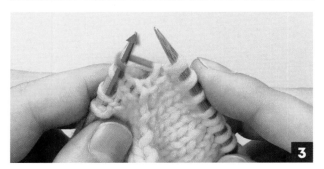

4. Knit into the new stitch by inserting the needle around the leftmost leg.

5. Wrap your yarn and complete the knit stitch.

MAKE 1 LEFT (M1L)

This increase will show up as a slight slant to the left.

1. Knit up to your increase point. Identify the strand of yarn between the last stitch you knit and the next stitch.

continued > > >

MAKE 1 LEFT (M1L) continued

2. Insert the working needle under the strand of yarn between your last knit stitch and the next stitch, putting it in from the back of your work to the front.

3. Pick up the strand with the working needle and place it on the other needle with the rightmost (forward) leg of the strand on the side of the needle facing you.

4. Knit into the new stitch by inserting the needle behind the rightmost leg.

5. Wrap your yarn and complete the knit stitch.

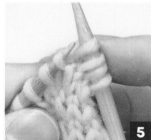

KNIT FRONT BACK

Knit front back, or kfb, is a simple and common increase stitch. This stitch leaves a small hole as it increases, making it best for fabric like garter or seed stitch, as opposed to stockinette where more seamless increases, like a make 1 left or make 1 right, are more in keeping with the fabric's texture.

1. Insert the needle into the desired stitch, as you would with any other knit stitch, coming from the front and going into the front leg of the stitch.

2. Yarn over and pull through with your working needle *but leave the stitch you just knit into on the opposite needle* (instead of pulling it off, as you normally would to finish the stitch).

3. Insert your working needle into the back leg of the same stitch you previously knit into, from the front to the back.

4. Yarn over and pull through with your working needle; now you can pull the stitch you just knit into off the other needle, to complete the increase stitch. You've just created two stitches where there was previously only one.

DECREASES

Like increases, decreases may be done in many ways. The most common decreases are the right-leaning knit 2 together and left-leaning slip slip knit. Like knit stitches, these decreases also have purl counterparts that are created by inserting your needle into the intended stitches from the opposite direction.

KNIT 2 TOGETHER (K2TOG)

1. Knit up to the decrease point. Insert the working needle into both of the next two stitches on the needle at the same time, going behind the front leg of the second stitch and then behind the front leg of the first stitch. (This is essentially knitting into two stitches as if they were one stitch.)

2. Wrap your yarn and complete the knit stitch.

SLIP SLIP KNIT (SSK)

1. Knit up to the decrease point. Insert the working needle behind the front leg of the first stitch of the other needle as if to knit, but pass the stitch onto the working needle without knitting into it. Repeat once more. You will now have two stitches from the previous row on your working needle; they should both have their frontmost leg on the left.

2. Insert the other needle (the one in your left hand) into both stitches by sliding it behind their frontmost legs; the needle will start at the back of the work and end up pointing out at the front of the work.

3. Wrap your yarn exactly the same way you do for a knit stitch and complete the decrease.

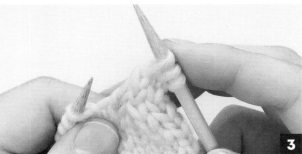

KNITTING IN THE ROUND

In many ways, knitting in the round is identical to knitting flat. The only notable difference is in the setup of casting on your stitches and knitting your first round. (A "round" is the same thing as a row.) Keep in mind that while knitting in the round, you will always be working on the right side of the work. This means that to create a stockinette stitch, you just knit every row. (If you want a garter stitch, you need to knit a row and then purl a row—exactly the opposite of what you'd do if you were knitting flat.)

1. Cast on your required number of stitches on circular needles or dispersed evenly on 3 to 4 double-pointed needles (DPNs). Move your cast-on stitches around the needles to space them evenly. Your working yarn should be on your working needle while the tail end of yarn should be on the other side of the loop, or row of DPNs. Be sure that your cast-on stitches are not twisted on the needles or the piece that connects them.

2. Hold your needles so that you've created a loop with the cast-on stitches; the working needle should be pointed at the slip knot you used to start casting on (that knot counts as your first cast-on stitch). Insert your working needle into that first slip knot/cast-on stitch, and either knit or purl that stitch, as indicated in the pattern.

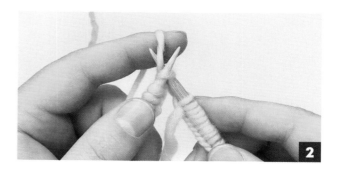

3. Knit or purl all the stitches around the loop, according to the pattern. When you have returned to the end of the round, you may place a stitch marker to indicate the beginning and end of rounds (this will help you keep track of how many rounds you've worked, and where they start and end).

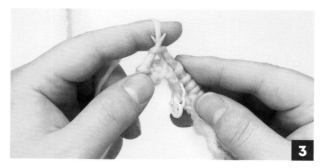

ADVANCED TECHNIQUES

There are hundreds, if not thousands, of techniques that you can come across as a knitter. And new techniques are being developed all the time. If you are ever curious about one or another, I encourage you to knit a swatch (a small 4- to 5-inch square of fabric) and try it out. It may be simpler than it seems. Here are two techniques that are often found in more sophisticated patterns.

LACE

Lace is a simple way to add beautiful texture to a piece; it also makes the fabric more breathable and lighter. There are many lace stitches that can be added to projects, but most include a combination of yarn overs (which make intentional open holes in the final fabric) and decreases. Every yarn over you make creates a new stitch with a little open hole below it and is paired with a decrease, which keeps the number of stitches in your knitting consistent. Let's look at the lace pattern created by the simple stitch repeat found in the Amethyst Lace Shawl (page 113) from Level 3 Patterns in this book.

1. Cast on the required number of stitches. Knit up to the lace section. Work a yarn over (yo): Wrap the working yarn around the working needle in a leftward motion, bringing it to the front of your work. (This loop of yarn, which is not connected to a knit stitch in the row below, will create a small, intentional hole in the fabric when you work into it in the following row.)

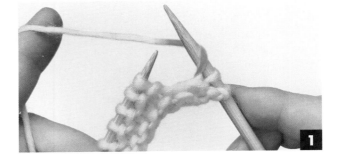

2. Decrease over the next two stitches with a purl 2 together (p2tog): Insert the working needle into the front strand of each of the next two stitches, as if to purl, and purl the two stitches together.

3. Repeat the process of working a yarn over, followed by purling two together, to the end of the section.

4. On the next row, work over all the stitches, treating each of the loops from the yarn overs as a full stitch. (Knitting or purling into these loops can feel tricky at first; make sure they don't fall off the needle, as they'll disappear and will look just like a loose strand in between stitches.)

PICKING UP AND KNITTING STITCHES

When you are working a seamed project with raw edges, you may need to pick up stitches around the raw edge and knit a border or band, such as a neckband. Thankfully, this is an easy skill and takes just a few simple steps.

1. Take your working needle and insert it between the outermost stitch and the next stitch in on the selvage edges. (On bound-off edges—on the back of the neckband, for example—the needle is inserted into the center of the stitch below the bind-off.)

2. Place new yarn over the end of your working needle.

3. Catching the new yarn, pull your working needle back through the side of the previous stitch, forming a new loop.

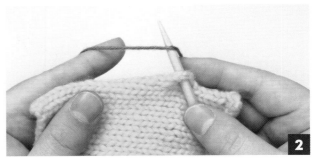

4. Continue picking up new evenly spaced stitches around your work according to how many stitches are required in your pattern. When complete, this will form your foundation row or round.

5. After completing the foundation, you will continue knitting as stated in the pattern.

PLACING STITCHES ON A HOLDER

In some patterns, live stitches need to be placed on a holder as you continue to knit other sections of the item you're making. This happens most often when a fabric that is knit in the round bisects into multiple sections, such as when you make the individual sleeves for sweaters or fingers for gloves. The process is simple, and although you can buy a dedicated stitch holder, you can also just use a yarn needle and waste yarn in a separate color.

1. Place the waste yarn on the yarn needle. Slip the number of stitches (stated in your pattern) from the needle with last round's stitches to the yarn needle and waste yarn.

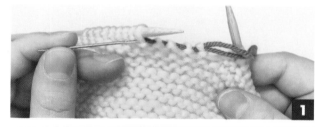

2. After all the stitches are on the waste yarn, tie the tails of waste yarn together and continue with the pattern.

CABLES

Cables are another way to add amazing texture and visual interest to your knits. Despite how complex they look, they are actually simple in practice. All cables follow the same basic construction: All you do is place some stitches from the left-hand needle onto a holder (most people use a cable needle, but you can also use a DPN), knit some stitches from the left-hand needle, then place the held stitches back onto the left-hand needle and knit them. The result is that those transferred stitches cross in front of the other stitches, creating a braided look that is called a cable. You can see this in action in the Garnet Cabled Fingerless Gloves (page 123) found in Level 3 Patterns in this book, where we use the same process.

1. Cast on the required number of stitches. Knit up to the cable instructions in the pattern. Slip the required number of stitches from the needle holding the stitches of the previous row onto a cable needle. (Here we're showing three stitches for each side of the cable, but you can use as many as called for in the pattern.)

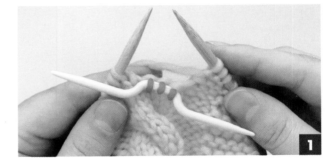

2. Move the cable needle with the stitches on it to the front of the work, and knit into the next workable stitch, skipping the stitches on the holder. Knit three stitches in total.

3. Place the stitches from the cable needle back onto the left-hand needle holding the stitches of the previous row on the left-hand needle in their original order.

4. Knit the three stitches normally, and complete the row as instructed in the pattern. Repeat this series of steps every few rows, as instructed in the pattern.

KNITTING INTO TWO STITCHES AT ONCE

When converting a piece of fabric that has been worked flat to a piece being worked in the round (as when you join the button band together for the Emerald Collared Raglan Pullover on page 127), sometimes you need an overlapped section of fabric. This overlap section strengthens the friction point, so that this part of the project doesn't stretch out over time. Working into two stitches at once creates this overlap. This reinforcement will produce one row that is slightly bulkier but will be unnoticeable on the right side. To do this, you will need a Double-Pointed Needle (DPN) about the same size as the other knitting needles you are working with.

1. Remove the required number of stitches from your working needle and place them onto a DPN.

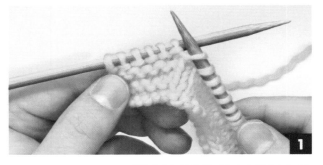

2. Place the DPN with its stitches behind the beginning stitches of your new round.

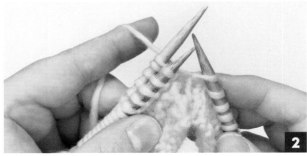

3. Insert your working needle into the first stitch of the new round and then into the first stitch on your DPN.

4. Wrap your yarn, as if to knit, and knit both stitches as one stitch.

5. Repeat steps 3 and 4 until there are no stitches left on your DPN.

6. Continue knitting as instructed.

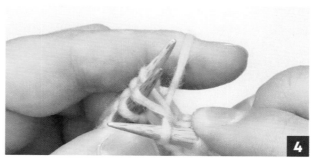

BINDING OFF AND CASTING ON MID-PROJECT

Sometimes you'll find that you're required to bind off and recast on while knitting a project. This can happen for a number of reasons, like when you're knitting button-holes or handles. The processes for binding off and casting on while still knitting use the same techniques as the methods we looked at earlier.

1. Begin by knitting up to your bind-off section. Bind off as many stitches as are required in the design, plus one stitch (see page 23). The loop on your working needle will count as your first stitch after the bind-off.

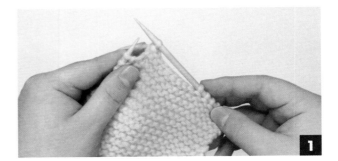

2. Finish knitting the row or round and compare the stitch count of the section to how many stitches remain on your needles. On the return row or round, cast on the required number of stitches when you get to the bind-off section using a short-tail cast-on (see page 22). Continue knitting as normal.

3. On the rows or rounds after the cast-on round, work your pattern as instructed.

FINISHING

After you've done the main work of knitting your pieces, you need to finish them. Finishing is just as important as the knitting itself. You've worked on a project for hours, even days, so you'll want it as presentable as possible. There are a few key finishing techniques to take into consideration when completing a project.

JOINING AND SEAMING

Sometimes pieces require seams, especially when you're knitting flat. There are many techniques out there that you can use when seaming, some less visible than others. One of the most common seams is the Mattress Stitch.

1. Place new yarn on a darning needle. The panels are positioned flat, right side up, and next to each other.

2. Pass the darning needle though the first stitch at the bottom of the intended seam line on either side or panel.

continued > > >

3. On the opposite side or panel, repeat the process of passing the darning needle through the first stitch exactly parallel to the previous first stitch.

4. Pass the darning needle through the stitch directly above the first stitch on the first panel.

5. Repeat the process of passing the darning needle through the stitch directly above the previous stitch on alternating sides.

6. Pull the yarn to tighten the seam after every 4 to 8 stiches. Once the seam is complete, trim the tails of yarn and weave in all the ends.

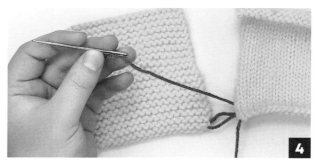

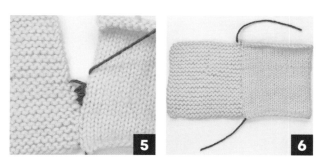

WEAVING IN ENDS

Weaving in ends is the most important finishing technique. This is the process of hiding all the yarn tails you've accumulated on a project. The objective when weaving in ends is not only to "hide" your tails, but also to make sure that they are secure and won't pop out after being worn or washed. Thankfully, this process is the same across all stitch types and is straightforward.

1. Thread the tail of yarn into the eye of a darning needle. Ideally, the yarn tail should be 4 to 5 inches in length. If the tail is on the right side of the work, pass the needle through to the wrong side.

2. Locate the closest stitch to the tail.

3. Pass your needle through the fabric in the same stitch, following the path of the stitch on the wrong side of the fabric.

4. Follow this row of stitches with your needle, weaving your tail into the fabric right alongside the same row for 5 to 7 stitches. Block the project before cutting the excess tail, ¼ inch away from the fabric.

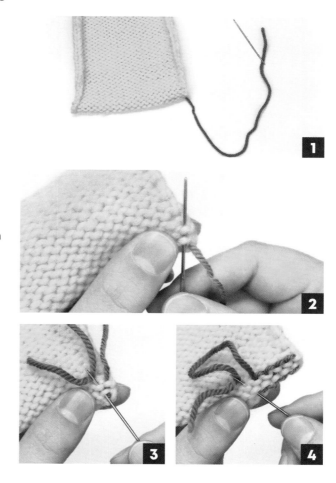

BLOCKING

Not every piece we make will be perfect right off the needles, and some pieces require you to manipulate the fabric into its intended shape. Blocking is a way to even out your stitches and gently stretch your projects to their desired finished dimensions by wetting them, pinning them to a mat, or a combination of both. There are three blocking styles that you can use: dry blocking, steam blocking, and wet blocking.

→ Dry blocking is useful when you need just a small bit of space. To dry block, place your piece flat on a mat. Gently stretch it to its intended size and pin around the edges to secure it in place while the stitches loosen and settle.

→ Steam blocking and wet blocking are helpful if an item needs to be stretched more than an inch or two. For steam blocking, use a steamer or an iron with a steam setting and steam the entire project on its front and back. If using an iron, do not touch the project directly with the iron, but instead hover the iron 2 to 3 inches away from the fabric. Lay the piece flat or pin it.

→ To prepare for wet blocking, submerge your project in room temperature or lukewarm water for 10 to 15 minutes (you can add leave-in detergent, like Soak or Eucalan), then gently wring it out and pat it dry with a towel before blocking. Lay the piece flat or pin it.

If your piece needs to be stretched a lot, or to a very specific shape, you can use pins (like T or fork pins) to secure your project into shape on a blocking mat, gently stretching it to its required dimensions. You can buy mats made for blocking, but I recommend buying interlocking foam pads from a hardware store. Leave all projects to block for at least six hours, or until fully dry if steam or wet blocking.

TASSELS, FRINGE, AND POM-POMS

These techniques are for making decorations, and they're definitely optional, but they can elevate a simple project into something more fun. You can get specially made tools for all three of these accents, but a thick piece of cardboard works well in a pinch.

TASSELS

1. Cut a piece of cardboard to the length you want your tassel to be. Wrap some yarn around the length of the cardboard 10 to 20 times. The more wraps, the fuller the tassel will be. Cut the yarn so it's no longer attached to the skein.

2. Cut a strand of yarn about 6 inches long and pass it between the wrapped yarn and the cardboard near one of the edges of the cardboard. Tie a square knot to cinch all the loops together.

continued > > >

3. Pull the wrapped yarn off the cardboard. Cut a strand of yarn about 6 inches long and tie it around the loops about ½ inch from the square knot. This is the top of your tassel.

4. Cut through all the loops at the opposite end—the bottom of the tassel.

5. Trim the finished tassel to the desired length.

FRINGE

1. Cut strands of working yarn that are twice as long as you want your fringe to be. You should have 1 to 3 strands of yarn per space or stitch you intend to add fringe to.

2. Fold the strands of yarn in half and insert a crochet hook into the spot you want to put the fringe, going from the right side of the fabric to the wrong side. Place the folded loops of yarn onto the crochet hook and pull them through the fabric just a little bit, so that the loop comes through but the ends of the yarn stay on the other side (this is your fringe).

3. Wrap the tail ends of the fringe yarn around the crochet hook as you would wrap yarn around a working needle while knitting. Pull the tail ends of fringe through the loop, and pull tight to secure the strands.

4. After all the fringe has been added, trim the fringe to a consistent length.

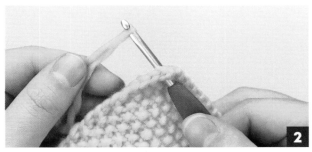

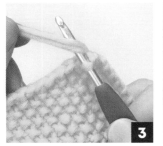

POM-POMS

1. Cut a piece of cardboard to the width you want your pom-pom to be, plus 1 inch. Wrap your yarn around the length of the cardboard 25 to 35 times. The more wraps, the fuller the pom-pom. Cut the yarn so it's no longer attached to the skein.

2. Cut a strand of new yarn to about 6 inches long. Carefully slide the wraps off the cardboard all together. With the new piece of yarn, tie a tight square knot directly in the middle of the wraps to cinch all the strands together.

3. Cut through the top of all the loops on either side of the knot.

4. While holding strands of new working yarn, fluff the pom-pom out and trim all the strands of yarn (except for the new working yarn) to a uniform length.

TROUBLESHOOTING

Everyone makes mistakes in their projects at one point or another. It's bound to happen. Most of the time, those mistakes are easily fixed. All it takes is a bit of knowledge and the proper techniques. Let's look at some of the problems beginners encounter most frequently and how to solve them.

Q: One of my stitches fell off my needles and it unraveled to a few rows down. How do I fix it?

A: This is what's known as a dropped stitch. Dropped stitches are the most common mistake and are thankfully simple to correct. How to fix a dropped stitch depends on whether you're knitting in garter or stockinette. If you've dropped stitches in a more complex stitch pattern, you may need to see the next question for further help.

STOCKINETTE/RIB

1. Take a crochet hook and insert it into the stitch you've dropped from the knit side—it's the loop at the bottom of the dropped stitch ladder from the front of the work to the back.

2. Place the dropped yarn from the row above the live stitch onto the crochet hook, above the dropped stitch, without twisting.

3. Pull the dropped yarn through the stitch (this works that first loop into the row above it, leaving you with an open loop in the next row up).

continued > > >

4. Repeat steps 2 and 3 until you reach the latest row of knitting, and place the live stitch onto the needle with the other live stitches from the previous row.

GARTER/SEED

1. Take your crochet hook and insert it into the live stitch at the bottom of the dropped stitch ladder from the knit side, from the front of the work to the back.

2. Place the dropped yarn from the row above the live stitch onto the crochet hook without twisting.

3. Pull the dropped yarn through the live stitch.
4. Gently remove the crochet hook and pass it through the live stitch from the opposite direction (you can turn your work upside down to make this easier).
5. Repeat steps 2 to 4 until you reach the latest row of knitting and place the live stitch onto the needle with the other live stitches from the previous row.

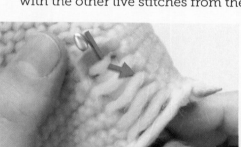

continued > > >

Q: I made a mistake a few rows down. Do I have to start all over?

A: Thankfully, no. You can, in fact, go as many rows back as you need (as long as it's not to the cast-on edge) to fix a mistake at any time. If the mistake is simple, like a single stitch or two, I'd recommend purposely dropping a stitch down to the problem area and fixing it as mentioned in the previous section.

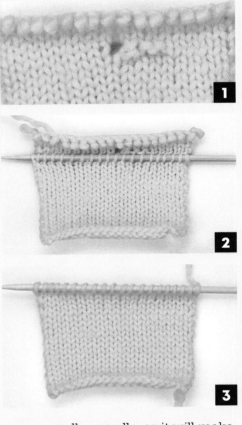

If there are multiple mistakes, especially with increases or decreases, the best way to correct it is to insert your needles into the row below the mistake and pull out just the rows above the mistake (this is also known as "ripping" or "frogging").

IDENTIFY THE PROBLEM ROW

1. Remove your needles from the row you are currently on.
2. Carefully insert your needle into each stitch of the row below the problem row, going through the leftmost leg of each stitch from the front of the work. You may wish to use a smaller needle, as it will make the process of going into the stitches easier.
3. Pull on the working yarn to unravel the rows above until you've ripped out everything above the row you inserted your needle intro. If your needle is in backward (the working yarn is on the wrong end), slip all stitches to the other needle. Start knitting from this row.

Q: I'm about to work a difficult section and am worried I may mess up. Is there something I can do as a safeguard in case I make mistakes, so I don't have to completely restart?

A: There is! You can insert a "lifeline." In essence, this functions the same way as inserting your needle into the fabric from the previous question and it holds a row steady, so that if you make a mistake, the knitting below the lifeline isn't affected.

When you are at the end of the row where you would like to insert your lifeline, cut a strand of smooth yarn in a contrasting yarn color 4 inches longer than the width of your project.

Place the contrasting yarn on a yarn needle and pass it through all the live stitches on your needle, directly under your needle. Be sure to have excess yarn on either edge.

Continue knitting as normal. If you make a mistake, you can take the live stitches off your needles and unravel all the stitches down to the lifeline. The stitches on your lifeline won't be ripped out because the yarn is holding on to them. Pass the needle through the live stitches directly under the lifeline.

Once all the stitches are on your needle, try the tricky part of the pattern again. If you complete your project and the lifeline is unneeded, simply pull out the lifeline from your fabric.

continued >>>

Q: I made a mistake a few stitches back. How can I go back and fix it?

A: Good job on spotting a mistake so quickly! It's much easier to fix these mistakes before they're 20 rows down. You will have to unknit (also called "tink") your stitches back to the problem area.

1. Identify the stitch below the newest stitch on your working needle. (This is the stitch you just knit into.)
2. Insert the needle with last row's live stitches (usually the one in your left hand) into that stitch.

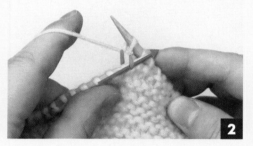

3. Pull the last stitch worked off your working needle and pull on the working yarn to unknit it.
4. Repeat steps 2 and 3 until you have unknit the mistake. Continue knitting as normal.

GLOSSARIES

STITCHES AND PATTERN INSTRUCTIONS

STITCH NAME	ABBREVIATION	DESCRIPTION	PAGE
Knit	k	Foundation stitch for knitting.	page 24
Purl	p	Foundation stitch for knitting; the exact opposite of the knit stitch.	page 29
Make 1 Right	m1r	Right-leaning inline knit increase stitch.	page 38
Make 1 Left	m1l	Left-leaning inline knit increase stitch.	page 39
Knit Front Back	kfb	Left-leaning pronounced knit increase stitch.	page 41
Knit 2 Together	k2tog	Right-leaning inline knit decrease stitch.	page 42
Purl 2 Together	p2tog	Right-leaning inline purl decrease stitch.	page 47
Slip Slip Knit	ssk	Left-leaning inline knit decrease stitch.	page 43
Yarn Over	yo	Lace increase stitch that leaves a purposeful hole in the fabric.	page 46
Cable 6 Front	c6f	Six-stitch-wide left-leaning knit cable pattern.	page 50–51
Right Side	RS	The front side of a project that is meant to be seen.	page 12
Parentheses	( )	Work instructions within parentheses as directed in the pattern.	page 11
Brackets	[ ]	Repeat instructions within brackets a set number of times as directed in the pattern.	page 11
Asterisk	*	Repeat instructions after asterisk (usually paired with parentheses) as directed in the pattern.	page 11

TECHNIQUES

NAME	DESCRIPTION	PAGE
Slip Knot	The beginning stitch of most cast-on types.	page 18
Cast-On	The foundation stitches of every knitting project. The two most common are the long-tail and short-tail cast-ons.	page 20
Bind-Off	The process of finishing your project by consecutively knitting the live stitches together until every stitch is knit off your needles and are interlocked.	page 23
Gauge	The number of stitches and rows of a fabric within a specified (usually 4 inches) measurement.	page 36
Blocking	The process of gently stretching your project to its specified measurements by means of wetting, pinning, or both.	page 58
Seaming	The process of stitching and joining together sections of your project (usually by means of a darning needle).	page 55
Weaving In Ends	The process of stitching the tail ends of yarn left on your project into the fabric of the work to secure and hide them.	page 57
Lace	Knitted fabric with decorative holes produced by working knits or purls in a pattern with yarn overs or other lace stitches.	page 46
Cables	Knitted fabric with decorative twists produced by knitting a handful of stitches out of order to manipulate the fabric.	page 50
Fringe	Accent yarn strands added onto projects after finishing (ex. on the ends of a scarf).	page 61
Pom-Poms	Accent tufts of yarn, usually spherical, added onto projects after finishing (ex. on the top of a beanie).	page 62
Tassels	Accent bundles of yarn added onto projects after finishing (ex. on the tips of a shawl).	page 59

NAME	DESCRIPTION	PAGE
Color Changes	The process of working in multiple colors of yarn within the same project as a design element.	page 28
Picking Up and Knitting Stitches	The process of working into prefinished fabric and pulling up new loops of yarn to knit from.	page 48
Placing Stitches on a Holder	The process of slipping live knit stitches from your needle onto waste yarn to be knit separately at another time.	page 49
Knitting into Two Stitches at Once	The process of working into two stitches from different sections of a project as one stitch to join both sections together.	page 52
Troubleshooting	The process of identifying and fixing mistakes within your knitted fabric.	page 63

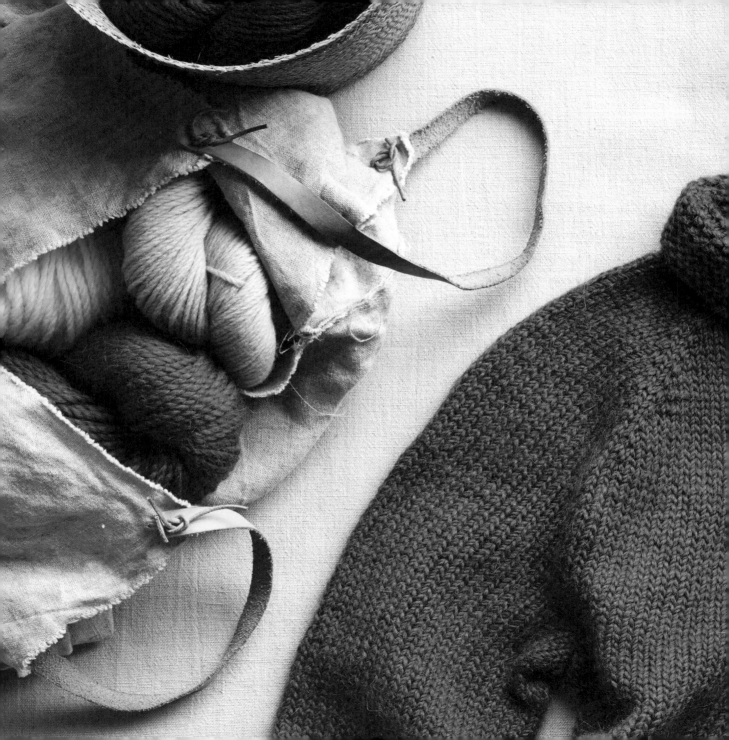

PART 2

Patterns

Now comes the fun part! After having worked through all those foundational instructions, you will have every skill required to knit all the patterns in this book—and thousands more. Let's get knitting.

Level 1 Patterns

Now that we have learned the basics of knitting, it's time to dive into real-world applications. In this level, we will focus on strengthening our knowledge and muscle memory for the basic stitch patterns. The patterns for these seven pieces are short and easy to memorize, so you can spend your time working on your form and discovering your personal rhythm, rather than reading and rereading the instructions. Because most of these pieces are flat, some are finished with the joining techniques discussed in part 1. If you would like to start with a join-free pattern, the Jasper Stitch Sampler Scarf (page 83) is the perfect introduction to this level. After working these seven projects, you will be more than ready to move on to level 2 patterns, which feature more in-the-round pieces and projects with increases and decreases.

STITCHES AND TECHNIQUES USED

Knit (k) (page 24)

Long-Tail Cast-On
(page 20)

Bind-Off (page 23)

Weaving In Ends
(page 57)

SIZE

About 8"/20 cm square

MATERIALS

◆ Paintbox Yarns Cotton Aran (100% cotton; 1.8 ounces/50 g = 93 yards/85 m): 1 skein in color Green Grass #630
◆ 9" straight needles US 8 (5.0 mm)
◆ Scissors
◆ Yarn needle

GAUGE

Gauge for this project is not critical.

16 stitches by 28 rows = 4" in garter

You're now ready to tackle your first project! When you work many rows of only knit stitches, the pattern that results—with raised ridges on both sides of the fabric—is called a garter stitch. This pattern uses this style's texture to full effect, because it's soft and absorbent. This garter stitch washcloth is the perfect item to start your knitting journey and makes an excellent gift around the holidays to add some handmade cheer.

INSTRUCTIONS

Cast on 32 sts.

Rows 1–56: K all sts.

Bind off and weave in ends **(see page 57).**

LAPIS CINCHED BEANIE

STITCHES AND TECHNIQUES USED

Knit (k) (page 24)

Purl (p) (page 29)

Long-Tail Cast-On
  (page 20)

Bind-Off (page 23)

Seaming (page 55)

Weaving In Ends (page 57)

Pom-Poms (page 62)

SIZE

Circumference:
  19½"/50 cm

Length: 8½"/22 cm

MATERIALS

◆ Knit Picks Swish
  Worsted (100% super-
  wash merino wool;
  1.8 ounces/50 g =
  110 yards/100 m):
  2 skeins in color Voyage
  Heather #28646
◆ 9" straight needles
  US 8 (5.0 mm)
◆ Scissors
◆ Yarn needle

GAUGE

20 stitches by 24 rows =
  4" in stockinette

This is the perfect beanie for beginner knitters. This hat is knit flat and uses just the rib stitch and stockinette stitch. Afterward, the hat is seamed together (see Joining and Seaming, page 55), then cinched closed at the top. You may also finish off the top of the hat with a pom-pom, if you'd like (see page 62).

INSTRUCTIONS

RIBBING

Cast on 98 stitches.

Row 1 (RS): K2 *(p2, k2) repeat from * to end of row.

Row 2: P2 *(k2, p2) repeat from * to end of row.

Rows 3–8: Repeat Rows 1 and 2.

BODY

Row 9: K all sts.

Row 10: P all sts.

Rows 11–50: Repeat Rows 9 and 10.

Bind off and weave in ends.

FINISHING

Fold the rectangle lengthwise, with the ribbing at the bottom and the right side (the smooth/knit side) facing out. Seam the raw side edges of the hat together (see Joining and Seaming, page 55). With a length of yarn and needle, loosely stitch around the top of the beanie using a simple running stitch. Take the tail and working end of yarn and tie them together in a square knot, cinching tightly to close the top of the beanie. Add a pom-pom to the top of the beanie, if desired. Weave in all ends.

PRACTICE PATTERN 3
RUBY IN-THE-ROUND COWL

STITCHES AND TECHNIQUES USED

Knit (k) (page 24)

Purl (p) (page 29)

Long-Tail Cast-On
   (page 20)

Bind-Off (page 23)

Weaving In Ends
   (page 57)

Knitting in the Round
   (page 44)

SIZE

Circumference:
   29½"/75 cm

Length: 8.75"/22 cm

MATERIALS

◆ Berroco Com-
   fort Worsted (50%
   acrylic, 50% nylon;
   3.5 ounces/100 g =
   210 yards/193 m):
   1 skein in color Pri-
   mary Red #9750
◆ 24" circular needles
   US 8 (5.0 mm)
◆ Scissors
◆ Yarn needle

This project will merge your mastery of knits and purls with an in-the-round construction. By the time you finish your cowl, you'll be confident in your ability to knit any style of item, whether flat or in the round. This cowl is a great wardrobe staple and could even work as a matching set for your brand-new beanie, with the right yarn color.

GAUGE
20 sts by 27 rounds = 4" in stockinette

INSTRUCTIONS
Cast on 148 sts in the round, careful not to twist.
Rounds 1–8 (RS): [K2, p2] *37 times.*
Rounds 9–52: K all sts.
Rounds 53–60: [K2, p2] *37 times.*
Bind off and weave in ends.

JASPER STITCH SAMPLER SCARF

STITCHES AND TECHNIQUES USED

Knit (k) (page 24)

Purl (p) (page 29)

Long-Tail Cast-On (page 20)

Bind-Off (page 23)

Weaving In Ends (page 57)

Fringe (page 61) (optional)

SIZE

Width: 6"/15 cm

Length: 100"/254 cm (without fringe)

MATERIALS

- Knit Picks Wonderfluff (70% baby alpaca, 7% merino wool, 23% nylon; 1.75 ounces/50 g = 142 yards/130 m): 3 balls in color Beehive Heather #29446
- 9" straight needles US 11 (8.0 mm)
- Scissors
- Yarn needle

This scarf helps you become familiar with working multiple stitch patterns all in one project. Working in segments, you will tackle seed stitch, garter, stockinette, and reverse stockinette. The result is an eye-catching scarf, and because of the nature and pairings of the stitch patterns, it's also 100 percent reversible.

GAUGE

13 stitches by 20 rows = 4" in pattern

INSTRUCTIONS

Cast on 19 stitches.

Row 1 (RS): K2, [p1, k1] seven times, p1, k2.

Rows 2–24: Repeat Row 1.

Row 25: K all sts.

Row 26: K2, p15, k2.

Rows 27–44: Repeat Rows 25 and 26.

Row 45: K all sts.

Rows 46–68: Repeat Row 45.

Row 69: K2, p15, k2.

Row 70: K all sts.

Rows 71–88: Repeat Rows 69 and 70.

Rows 89–440: Repeat Rows 1–88 four times.

Rows 441–508: Repeat Rows 1–68.

Bind off and weave in ends.

FINISHING (OPTIONAL)

Add 3 to 4 inches of fringe to the cast-on and bind-off edges.

MARBLE RIB PILLOWCASE

STITCHES AND TECHNIQUES USED

Knit (k) (page 24)
Purl (p) (page 29)
Long-Tail Cast-On
   (page 20)
Bind-Off (page 23)
Seaming (page 55)
Weaving In Ends
   (page 57)

SIZE

15"/38 cm square

MATERIALS

◆ Paintbox Yarns Wool
   Mix Super Chunky
   (50% wool, 50% acrylic;
   3.5 ounces/100 g
   = 60 yards/55 m):
   4 skeins in color Misty
   Grey #903
◆ 16" pillow insert
◆ 9" straight needles
   US 11 (8.0 mm)
◆ Scissors
◆ Yarn needle

GAUGE

10 stitches by 14 rows =
   4" in 2x2 ribbing

This pillowcase is a great way to practice the rib stitch. It's worked as a single flat rectangle. When you're done knitting, you only need to sew up two seams to finish it, with an opening in the middle back to easily slip your pillow insert in and out. This style of construction allows the pillowcase to be swapped out and laundered, if needed.

INSTRUCTIONS

Cast on 40 sts.
Row 1 (RS): K3, [p2, k2] *nine times*, k1.
Row 2: P3, [k2, p2] *nine times*, p1.
Rows 3–112: Repeat Rows 1 and 2.
Bind off and weave in all ends.

FINISHING

Place the panel flat with the right side facing down and the short end of the rectangle facing you. Fold over both short ends (the bottom of the rectangle folds up, and the top folds down) so they meet up in the center of the rectangle, then overlap them by 1 inch. (The panel should have the overlapping edges in the middle of the work, and the right side will now be facing out.) With some of your leftover yarn and a darning needle, seam both of the open side edges closed, leaving the middle overlapping short edges unseamed. This overlap is where you'll put the pillow in and will be the back of your project. Weave in all ends and insert the pillow.

RUBELLITE STOCKINETTE HEADBAND

This headband is a great way to practice flat stockinette stitch. The main band and the cinch are both worked as flat rectangles, then seamed into tubes to create a chic and interesting headband everyone is sure to love.

STITCHES AND TECHNIQUES USED

Knit (k) (page 24)

Purl (p) (page 29)

Long-Tail Cast-On (page 20)

Bind-Off (page 23)

Seaming (page 55)

Weaving In Ends (page 57)

Knitting Two Yarns Together (page 37)

SIZE

Circumference: 21"/53 cm

Width: 3"/8 cm

MATERIALS

◆ Berroco Ultra Wool Worsted (100% superwash merino wool; 3.5 ounces/100 g = 219 yards/200 m): 1 skein in color Hibiscus #3331

MATERIALS (CONT.)

◆ Berroco Aerial (65% superkid mohair, 35% silk; 0.9 ounces/25 g = 284 yards/260 m): 1 ball in color Magenta #3457
◆ 9" straight needles US 8 (5.0 mm)
◆ Scissors
◆ Yarn needle

GAUGE

18 stitches by 24 rows = 4" in stockinette with both yarns held together

> ⊁NOTE⊰ Hold and work both yarns together as one yarn throughout the project.

INSTRUCTIONS

FOR THE HEADBAND

Cast on 30 sts.

Row 1 (RS): K all sts.

Row 2: P all sts.

Rows 3–124: Repeat Rows 1 and 2.

Row 125: K all sts.

Bind off and weave in ends. Set aside.

continued > > >

FOR THE CINCH

Cast on 18 sts.
Row 1 (RS): K all sts.
Row 2: P all sts.
Rows 3–20: Repeat Rows 1 and 2.
Bind off and weave in ends.

FINISHING

Lay the headband piece flat with the right side facing down. Fold it in half length-wise, so the right side is on the outside, and the wrong sides are facing together to form a long tube. With some of your leftover yarn and a darning needle, seam the two long edges of the headband together to form a long open tube. Next, seam together the two open ends of the stockinette tube to form the headband shape.

Take the cinch panel and seam it lengthwise into a second, smaller open tube, using the same steps outlined on page 55.

Roll the headband tube so that the long seam is on the inside of the headband. Take the unfinished cinch tube and wrap it around the seam where the short ends of the headband tube are seamed together. Seam the open ends of the cinch tube together over the headband's seam (to hide it) and rotate the cinch band's seam to the inside of the headband. Weave in all ends and block to finish.

SAPPHIRE GARTER BAG

STITCHES AND TECHNIQUES USED

Knit (k) (page 24)

Long-Tail Cast-On
  (page 20)

Short-Tail Cast-On
  (page 22)

Binding-Off and Casting-
  On Mid-Project
  (page 54)

Bind-Off (page 23)

Weaving In Ends
  (page 57)

Knitting Two Yarns
  Together (page 37)

SIZE

11"/28 cm square

MATERIALS

◆ Berroco Modern
  Cotton (60%
  Pima cotton, 40%
  modal rayon;
  3.5 ounces/100 g =
  209 yards/191 m):
  2 hanks in color
  India Point #1690

This bag is a great introduction to binding off and casting on stitches mid-project. (There is a tutorial for this skill on page 54.) To construct this bag, you will knit two square panels of the same size. However, before you finish each square, you will cast off stitches in the middle of a row and cast on additional stitches on the return row, to form an opening that will be used as the handle. When you've finished the two squares, you will seam them together to finish.

MATERIALS (CONT.)

◆ Berroco Dulce (50% cotton, 20% nylon, 16% alpaca,
  14% wool; 1.75 ounces/50 g = 175 yards/160 m): 2 balls
  in color Sapphire #2022
◆ 9" straight needles US 6 (4.0 mm)
◆ Scissors
◆ Yarn needle

GAUGE

18 stitches by 28 rows = 4" in garter with both yarns
  held together

》**NOTE**《 Hold and work both yarns together and use them as one yarn throughout the project.

continued > > >

SAPPHIRE GARTER BAG continued

INSTRUCTIONS

PANELS (MAKE 2)

Cast on 60 stitches.

Rows 1–10: K all sts.

Row 11: K15, bind off 30 sts, k15. [30 stitches on needle at end of row]

Row 12: K15, cast on 20 sts using short-tail cast-on (see tutorial on page 22), k15.
    [50 sts on the needle]

Rows 13–78: K all sts.

Bind off and weave in ends.

FINISHING

Block panels to the finished dimensions specified on page 91. With some of your left-over yarn and a darning needle, seam the sides and bottom of the panels together to form a bag. (The top end, which is the cast-on edge, stays open. This is the one closest to the openings you'll use as handles.) Weave in all ends.

Level 2 Patterns

Congratulations on completing the level 1 patterns! You are well on your way to mastering the art of knitting. Now we can bring in more simple and effective techniques, like striping, knitting in the round, and increases and decreases. In these level 2 patterns, you will find projects like a scarf, clutch, and baby blanket, which all make use of simple increasing and decreasing techniques to create interesting shapes. There is also an in-the-round baby- and child-size hat pattern that is sure to provide a fun and manageable challenge. By the end of this level, you will have all the practice you need to begin work on more advanced skills, like garments, cables, and lace.

QUARTZ BIAS SCARF

STITCHES AND TECHNIQUES USED

Knit (k) (page 24)
Slip Slip Knit (ssk)
   (page 43)
Knit Front Back (kfb)
   (page 41)
Long-Tail Cast-On
   (page 20)
Bind-Off (page 23)
Weaving In Ends
   (page 57)
Fringe (page 61)
   (optional)

SIZE

Width: 4½"/11 cm
Length: 110"/279 cm

MATERIALS

◆ Noro Kureyon (100%
   wool; 1.75 ounces/50 g
   = 110 yards/100 m):
   5 skeins in color
   Hida #319
◆ 9" straight needles
   US 8 (5.0 mm)
◆ Scissors
◆ Yarn needle

This scarf is knit with strategically placed increases and decreases to create a fabric that is worked on the bias, or diagonally. While working this project, you will strengthen your increasing and decreasing skills and learn a new increase stitch. (There is a tutorial for this skill on page 41.) The main fabric is simple and easy to knit, and the shaping and fabric manipulation adds a fun and interesting challenge.

GAUGE

16 stitches by 24 rows = 4" in garter

> **TIP:** Because this piece is knit diagonally, the length and width of the piece are not directly correlated to the gauge of the project. As you work your scarf, if you feel it is too thin or wide, restart and add or decrease stitches in multiples of four at the cast on.

INSTRUCTIONS

Cast on 30 sts.
Row 1: K all sts.
Row 2: Kfb (see tutorial on page 41), k27, ssk.
Rows 3–580: Repeat Rows 1 and 2.
Bind off and weave in ends.

FINISHING (OPTIONAL)

Add 3 to 4 inches of fringe to the cast-on and bind-off edges.

AGATE SEED STITCH CLUTCH

STITCHES AND TECHNIQUES USED

Knit (k) (page 24)
Purl (p) (page 29)
Slip Slip Knit (ssk)
    (page 43)
Knit 2 Together (k2tog)
    (page 42)
Long-Tail Cast-On
    (page 20)
Bind-Off (page 23)
Seaming (page 55)
Weaving In Ends
    (page 57)
Knitting Two Yarns
    Together (page 37)

SIZE

Width: 9"/23 cm
Depth: 6"/15 cm
    (after seaming)

MATERIALS

◆ Berroco Chai (56%
    linen, 44% silk;
    1.75 ounces/50 g =
    142 yards/130 m):
    2 balls each in colors
    Delft #8626 and
    Coconut #8600

This clutch is constructed flat in one piece. After it is knit, the sides are seamed closed to form the bag. The unique shape is created by first knitting a flat rectangle, then slowly tapering the front of the bag to a triangular point, which becomes the purse flap when the project is sewn up.

◆ 9" straight needles
    US 5 (3.75 mm)

MATERIALS (CONT.)

◆ Chain strap
◆ Scissors
◆ Yarn needle

GAUGE

18 stitches by 28 rows = 4" in seed stitch with both yarns
    held together

>NOTE< Hold and work both yarns together as one yarn throughout the project.

INSTRUCTIONS

Cast on 41 stitches.
Rows 1–90 (RS): [K1, p1] to 1 st from end of row, k1.
Row 91: Ssk, [k1, p1] to 3 sts from end of row, k1, k2tog.
    [39 stitches on needle at end of row]
Row 92: [P1, k1] to 1 st from end of row, p1.

continued > > >

Row 93: Ssk, [p1, k1] to 3 sts from end of row, p1, k2tog. [37 sts on needle]
Row 94: [K1, p1] to 1 st from end of row, K1.
Rows 95–128: Repeat Rows 91–94. [end with 3 sts on needle]
Bind off and weave in ends.

FINISHING

On the right side of the fabric, fold over from the beginning row up to row 90 right before decrease shaping begins. With new yarn and a darning needle, seam both side edges closed. Weave in all ends.

AMBER C2C BABY BLANKET

STITCHES AND TECHNIQUES USED

Knit (k) (page 24)

Yarn Over (yo) (page 46)

Knit 2 Together (k2tog) (page 42)

Long-Tail Cast-On (page 20)

Bind-Off (page 23)

Seaming (page 55)

Weaving In Ends (page 57)

SIZE

35"/89 cm square

MATERIALS

- Knit Picks Snuggle Puff (70% cotton, 30% nylon; 1.75 ounces/50 g = 142 yards/130 m): 6 balls in color Owlet #28795
- 9" straight needles, 24" circular needles US 10 (6.0 mm)
- Scissors
- Yarn needle

This corner-to-corner (c2c) garter stitch baby blanket is a new take on a classic motif. The c2c square is a staple project in any knitter's handbook, but this one has a new twist: Additional increase rows are knit after the body is completed. The extra section created by these increases is folded over and seamed to the body, making a pocket that the blanket can be folded into when it's not in use. It also makes for a handy pillow.

GAUGE

13 stitches by 26 rows = 4" in garter

> **NOTE** Switch from 9-inch straight needles to 24-inch circular needles when stitches can no longer comfortably fit on straight needles. Continue knitting flat with circular needles, as if knitting with straight needles.

INSTRUCTIONS

Cast on 5 stitches.

Rows 1–3: K all sts.

Row 4: K2, yo, k to end of row. [6 sts on needle at end of row]

Rows 5–158: Repeat Row 4. [end with 160 sts on needle]

Row 159: K1, k2tog, yo, k2tog, k to end of row. [159 sts on needle]

continued > > >

Rows 160–311: Repeat Row 159. [end with 7 sts on needle]
Row 312: K2, yo, k to end of row. [8 sts on needle]
Rows 313–362: Repeat Row 312. [58 sts on needle]
Rows 363–368: K all sts.
Bind off and weave in ends.

FINISHING

Fold along row 312 where the body of the blanket comes to a point. With some of your remaining yarn and a darning needle, seam both diagonal edges together, leaving the middle space unseamed. Block the blanket to the finished dimensions noted on page 103. Weave in all ends.

 To convert the blanket to a pillow, fold in all three regular corners and tuck the fabric into the pocket formed by the folded corner.

OPAL STRIPED CHILDREN'S BEANIE

SIZE

Circumference: 11¼ (13¼,
  14½, 16¾)"/28.5 (33.5, 37,
  42.5) cm

Height: 5 (6, 7, 7¾)"/12.5
  (15, 18, 19.5) cm

This multi-size beanie is a great intro project for in-the-round work and manual striping of yarns. It also introduces the concept of different sizing options within the same pattern and can be made to fit an infant through adolescent.

MATERIALS

- Wool of the Andes Superwash Worsted (100% super-wash wool; 1.75 ounces/50 g = 110 yards/100 m): 1 skein each in colors **A** Oyster Heather #26317, **B** Celestial #26335, **C** Semolina #26329, **D** Rogue #26333
- DPNs in US 6 (4.0 mm)
- 4 stitch markers
- Scissors
- Yarn needle

GAUGE

23 stitches by 28 rows = 4" in stockinette

> **›NOTE‹** You will change yarn colors every 7 rounds, starting with yarn A, and moving in alphabetical order, starting over again after D.

continued › › ›

OPAL STRIPED CHILDREN'S BEANIE continued

TIP: What are the numbers in parentheses in the size guide on page 107 and in the following pattern? These are sizing option instructions. You will work the pattern as normal, and when you run into a section with these options, you will always select the option for your preferred size. For example, if you want to make a beanie with a 14½-inch circumference, it is the third option listed. That means it will also be 7 inches in height, as that is the third height option. In that case, every time you encounter these parentheses in the instructions, you will follow the number or round count of the third option. It may help to highlight or underline your chosen option every time it comes up in the pattern before starting.

INSTRUCTIONS

Cast on 64 (76, 84, 96) sts.

Rounds 1–6: K2, p2 around. [64 (76, 84, 96) stitches on needle at end of round]

Round 7: [K16 (19, 21, 24), pm] *four times.* This is where you change color for the first time; see note on page 107.

Rounds 8–22 (27, 32, 35): K around.

Round 23 (28, 33, 34): [Ssk, k to 2 sts before next marker, k2tog, sm] *four times.* [56 (68, 76, 88) sts on needle]

Round 24 (29, 34, 35): K all sts.

Rounds 25 (30, 35, 36)–34 (41, 48, 53): Repeat Rounds 23 (28, 33, 34) and 24 (29, 34, 35). [end with 16 (20, 20, 16) sts on needle]

Round 35 (42, 49, 54): Repeat Round 23 (28, 33, 34). [8 (12, 12, 8) sts on needle]

Cut yarn, leaving a 4-inch tail. Draw tails through the remaining stitches, pull tight to close, and fasten off. Weave in all ends.

FINISHING (OPTIONAL)

Add a multicolored pom-pom on top of the beanie, or two pom-poms to the sides as ears.

Level 3 Patterns

By this point in the book, if you've been taking things step-by-step and pattern-by-pattern, you can consider yourself an intermediate knitter! We have worked through eleven increasingly complex designs, and now we come to our most advanced projects. These final four projects will cover the remaining styles and skills you'll find in the kinds of knitting projects most hobby knitters are using. This includes techniques like making lace and cables as well as garment construction. We will walk through each new technique with step-by-step tutorials so that you will be able to make these items with confidence and finish this book feeling secure in your newfound knitting skills.

AMETHYST LACE SHAWL

SIZE

Wingspan: 54"/137 cm

Depth: 42"/107 cm

MATERIALS

◆ Berroco Ultra Alpaca
   (50% superfine alpaca,
   50% Peruvian wool;
   3.5 ounces/100 g =
   219 yards/200 m):
   4 hanks in color
   Orchid #6267

This shawl showcases a simple triangular construction and features a simple repeating lace pattern. Oversized tassels adorn each of the three points to add to the drape of this beautiful layering piece. By the end of this project, you will have a clear understanding of lace basics. The project will also help you strengthen your row counting skills, because you will need to work increase rows at odd intervals.

MATERIALS (CONT.)

◆ 14" straight needles and/or 24" to 36" circular needles
   US 9 (5.5 mm)
◆ Scissors
◆ Yarn needle
◆ Locking stitch marker

> ⟩NOTE⟨ Place the locking stitch marker on each increase row as you knit to better track where your next increase row is worked.

GAUGE

10 stitches by 20 rows = 4" in lace pattern

INSTRUCTIONS

Cast on 6 sts.

Rows 1, 2: K all sts.

Row 3: K2, kfb *two times*, k2. [8 stitches on needle at
   end of row]

continued > > >

Rows 4, 5: K all sts.
Row 6: K3, kfb *two times*, k3. [10 sts on needle]
Rows 7, 8: K4, yo, p2tog, k4.
Row 9: K3, kfb, yo, p2tog, kfb, k3. [12 sts on needle]
Rows 10, 11: K5, yo, p2tog, k5.
Row 12: K4, kfb, yo, p2tog, kfb, k4. [14 sts on needle]
Rows 13, 14: K4, [yo, p2tog] *three times*, k4.
Row 15: K3, kfb, [yo, p2tog] *until 4 sts from end of row*, kfb, k3. [16 sts on needle]
Rows 16, 17: K5, [yo, p2tog] *until 5 sts from end of row*, k5.
Row 18: K4, kfb, [yo, p2tog] *until 5 sts from end of row*, kfb, k4. [18 sts on needle]
Rows 19, 20: K4, [yo, p2tog] *until 4 sts from end of row*, k4.
Rows 21–200: Repeat Rows 15–20. [end with 138 sts on needle]
Row 201: K3, kfb, k to 4 sts from end of row, kfb, k3. [140 sts on needle]
Rows 202–207: K all sts.
Bind off and weave in ends.

FINISHING (OPTIONAL)

Create three dense tassels 5 to 6 inches long, then attach one to each of the three points of the shawl. Steam or wet blocking is highly encouraged for all lace projects.

CITRINE BABY BASKETWEAVE VEST

STITCHES AND TECHNIQUES USED

Knit (k) (page 24)

Purl (p) (page 29)

Slip Slip Knit (ssk)
(page 43)

Knit 2 Together (k2tog)
(page 42)

Long-Tail Cast-On
(page 20)

Bind-Off (page 23)

Knitting in the Round
(page 44)

Picking Up and Knitting
Stitches (page 48)

Placing Stitches on a
Holder (page 49)

Seaming (page 55)

Weaving In Ends
(page 57)

SIZE

Finished Chest
Circumference: 17
(18, 19, 20, 21)"/43
(46, 48, 51, 53) cm

A pattern of knits and purls on the body of this baby vest forms a basketweave pattern. This pattern is the perfect intro level project for simple garment construction. Because this piece is small, it gives you an opportunity to learn the basics of knitting a seamed garment without being intimidated. Making this vest will also teach you how to pick up stitches on a finished panel. (There is a tutorial for this skill on page 48.)

MATERIALS

◆ Paintbox Yarns Baby DK (45% acrylic, 55% nylon; 1.75 ounces/50 g = 183 yards/167 m): 1 (2, 2, 2, 2) skein in color Buttercup Yellow #722
◆ 9" straight needles US 6 (4 mm)
◆ DPNs US 4 (3.5 mm)
◆ Scissors
◆ Yarn needle

GAUGE

20 stitches by 30 rows = 4" in stockinette

INSTRUCTIONS

BACK PANEL

Cast on 42 (44, 48, 50, 52) stitches with straight needles.
Rows 1–8 (RS): [K1, p1] across all sts.
Row 9: K5 (6, 4, 5, 6), [p4, k4] *4 (4, 5, 5, 5) times,* p5 (6, 4, 5, 6).
Rows 10–14: Repeat Row 9.

continued > > >

Row 15: P5 (6, 4, 5, 6), [k4, p4] *4 (4, 5, 5, 5) times,* k5 (6, 4, 5, 6).
Rows 16–20: Repeat Row 15.
Rows 21–44: Repeat Rows 9–20.
Row 45: K all sts.
Row 46: P all sts.
Rows 47–74 (78, 82, 86, 90): Repeat Rows 45 and 46.
Bind off and weave in ends.

FRONT PANEL
Cast on 42 (44, 48, 50, 52) stitches with straight needles.
Rows 1–8 (RS): [K1, p1] across all sts.
Row 9: K5 (6, 4, 5, 6), [p4, k4] *4 (4, 5, 5, 5) times,* p5 (6, 4, 5, 6).
Rows 10–14: Repeat Row 9.
Row 15: P5 (6, 4, 5, 6), [k4, p4] *4 (4, 5, 5, 5) times,* k5 (6, 4, 5, 6).
Rows 16–20: Repeat Row 15.
Rows 21–44: Repeat Rows 9–20.
Row 45: K all sts.
Row 46: P all sts.
Rows 47–50 (54, 56, 60, 62): Repeat Rows 45 and 46.

LEFT NECK SHAPING
Row 51 (55, 57, 61, 63): K19 (20, 22, 23, 24), k2tog, place remaining sts of row on waste yarn. [20 (21, 23, 24, 25) stitches on needle at end of row]
Row 52 (56, 58, 62, 64): P all sts.
Row 53 (57, 59, 63, 65): K to 2 sts before end of row, k2tog. [19 (20, 22, 23, 24) sts on needle]
Row 54 (58, 60, 64, 66): P all sts.
Rows 55 (59, 61, 65, 67)–70 (74, 78, 82, 86): Repeat Rows 53 (57, 59, 63, 65) and 54 (58, 60, 64, 66). [end with 11 (12, 13, 14, 14) sts on needle]

Row 71 (75, 79, 83, 87): K all sts.

Row 72 (76, 80, 84, 88): P all sts.

Rows 73 (77, 81, 85, 89)–74 (78, 82, 86, 90): Repeat Rows 71 (75, 79, 83, 87) and 72 (76, 80, 84, 88).

Bind off and weave in ends.

RIGHT NECK SHAPING

Remove any waste yarn and place the needle back into live sts in the previous position. Begin the next row in new yarn.

Row 51 (55, 57, 61, 63): Ssk, k to end of row. [20 (21, 23, 24, 25) sts on needle]

Row 52 (56, 58, 62, 64): P all sts.

Rows 53 (57, 59, 63, 65)–70 (74, 78, 82, 86): Repeat Rows 51 (55, 57, 61, 63) and 52 (56, 58, 62, 64). [end with 11 (12, 13, 14, 14) sts on needle]

Row 71 (75, 79, 83, 87): K all sts.

Row 72 (76, 80, 84, 88): P all sts.

Rows 73 (77, 81, 85, 89)–74 (78, 82, 86, 90): Repeat Rows 71 (75, 79, 83, 87) and 72 (76, 80, 84, 88).

Bind off and weave in ends.

JOINING

With yarn needle and new yarn, seam the tops of the front and back panels together. There will be an unseamed section along the top of the back panel, which is the back neck edge. Join both side seams of the vest from cast-on edges up to row 40 (44, 44, 48, 48). Bind off and weave in ends.

continued > > >

NECKBAND

With new yarn and your DPNs, pick up and knit 69 (69, 75, 75, 81) sts around the neck hole (see Picking Up and Knitting Stitches tutorial, page 48), starting by picking up 1 stitch at the middle point of the front panel, followed by 24 (24, 26, 26, 28) stitches along the left front neck, 20 (20, 22, 22, 24) stitches along the back neck, and 24 (24, 26, 26, 28) stitches along the right front neck.

Rounds 1, 2: [K1, p1] around until 1 st from end of round, k1.

Round 3: Ssk, [k1, p1] around until 2 sts from end of round, k2tog. [67 (67, 73, 73, 79) sts on needle]

Rounds 4, 5: K2, [p1, k1] until 1 st from end of round, k1.

Round 6: Ssk, [p1, k1] until 3 sts from end of round, p1, k2tog. [65 (65, 71, 71, 77) sts on needle]

Bind off and weave in ends.

SHOULDER BANDS (MAKE 2)

With DPNs, beginning at the side seam, pick up and knit 68 (68, 76, 76, 84) sts evenly around the raw shoulder edge.

Rounds 1–5: [K1, p1] around.

Bind off and weave in ends. Block according to the finished measurements.

MEASUREMENTS

Chest Circumference **A**: 17 (18, 19, 20, 21)"/43 (46, 48, 51, 53) cm

Length **B**: 9.75 (10½, 11, 11½, 12)"/25 (26.5, 28, 29, 30.5) cm

Neck **C**: 4 (4, 4½, 4½, 4¾)"/10 (10, 11.5, 11.5, 12) cm

GARNET CABLED FINGERLESS GLOVES

STITCHES AND TECHNIQUES USED

Knit (k) (page 24)

Purl (p) (page 29)

Knit 2 Together (k2tog) (page 42)

Slip Slip Knit (ssk) (page 43)

Make 1 Right (m1r) (page 38)

Make 1 Left (m1l) (page 39)

Cable 6 Front (c6f)

Long-Tail Cast-On (page 20)

Short-Tail Cast-On (page 22)

Bind-Off (page 23)

Knitting in the Round (page 44)

Picking Up and Knitting Stitches (page 48)

Placing Stitches on a Holder (page 49)

Cables (page 50)

Weaving In Ends (page 57)

SIZE

Length: 8½"/22 cm

Circumference: 6"/15 cm unstretched to 10"/25 cm stretched

These simple fingerless gloves are the perfect intro project to cable work. In this bite-size project, you will become familiar with simple cabling, knitting a thumb gusset, and placing stitches on a waste yarn so that you can come back to knit them later. (There is a tutorial for this skill on page 49.) If your knitting has become relatively fast and fluid, a single pair of these gloves can easily be made in a day, making this a perfect knitting pattern to have handy for a quick handmade gift.

MATERIALS

- Berroco Lanas (100% wool; 3.5 ounces/ 100 g = 219 yards/200 m): 1 skein in color Cayenne #95126
- DPNs US 10 (6.0 mm)
- Cable needle
- Scissors
- Yarn needle

GAUGE

21 stitches by 21 rows = 4" in 3x3 ribbing, unstretched

INSTRUCTIONS

GLOVES (MAKE 2)

Cast on 45 stitches in the round, being careful not to twist.

continued > > >

Rounds 1–20: [K3, p3] *five times*, k6, p3, k3, p3.
Round 21: [K3, p3] *five times*, c6f, p3, k3, p3.
Rounds 22–25: [K3, p3] *five times*, k6, p3, k3, p3.
Rounds 26–30: Repeat Rounds 21–25.
Round 31: Repeat Round 21.

RIGHT GLOVE GUSSET
Round 32: K1, m1r, k1, m1l, k1, p3, [k3, p3] *four times*, k6, p3, k3, p3. [47 stitches on needle at end of round]
Round 33: K2, m1r, k1, m1l, k2, p3, [k3, p3] *four times*, k6, p3, k3, p3. [49 sts on needle]
Round 34: K3, m1r, k1, m1l, k3, p3, [k3, p3] *four times*, k6, p3, k3, p3. [51 sts on needle]
Round 35: Cast on 3 sts using short-tail cast-on, slip 9 sts onto waste yarn (see tutorial on page 49), p3, [k3, p3] *four times*, k6, p3, k3, p3. [45 sts on needle]

LEFT GLOVE GUSSET
Round 32: [K3, p3] *three times*, k1, m1r, k1, m1l, k1, p3, k3, p3, k6, p3, k3, p3. [47 sts on needle]
Round 33: [K3, p3] *three times*, k2, m1r, k1, m1l, k2, p3, k3, p3, k6, p3, k3, p3. [49 sts on needle]
Round 34: [K3, p3] *three times*, k3, m1r, k1, m1l, k3, p3, k3, p3, k6, p3, k3, p3. [51 sts on needle]
Round 35: [K3, p3] *three times*, cast on 3 sts using short-tail cast-on, slip 9 sts onto waste yarn, p3, k3, p3, k6, p3, k3, p3. [45 sts on needle]

BOTH GLOVES
Rounds 36–45: Repeat Rounds 21–25.
Bind off and weave in ends.

THUMB
Place all 9 sts from the waste yarn onto 3 DPNs. Divide the sts evenly between the needles. With a fourth DPN and new yarn, pick up and knit 5 sts around the top of the thumb hole where the 3 sts were cast on. There will be 14 sts on your needles.
Round 1: K9, k2tog, k1, ssk. [12 sts on needle]
Rounds 2–5: K12.
Rounds 6, 7: [K1, p1] *six times.*
Bind off and weave in ends.

EMERALD COLLARED RAGLAN PULLOVER

This final pattern is a raglan-style adult sweater knit from the top down. It appears sophisticated but is easy to do and will be a snap if you've already worked through the patterns earlier in this book. You begin this sweater by knitting flat, then you join the pieces to work in the round by knitting into two stitches together; I've provided a tutorial for this technique on page 52. Afterward, the sweater is constructed in a traditional raglan style, meaning that increases along the top of the sweater occur at four fixed points. To finish, stitches are picked up along the cast-on edge and a collar is knit.

SIZE

Chest Circumference: 36 (40, 44, 48, 52, 56, 60, 64)"/91
(102, 112, 122, 132, 142, 152, 162) cm

MATERIALS

- Berroco Ultra Alpaca Chunky (50% superfine alpaca, 50% Peruvian wool; 3.5 ounces/100 g = 131 yards/120 m): 6 (7, 7, 8, 8, 9, 10, 11) hanks in color Emerald Mix #72184
- 16", 24", 32" circular needles in US 8 (5.0 mm)
- 1 DPN around size US 8 (5.0 mm)
- 4 stitch markers
- 2 (²/₃" to 1") buttons
- Scissors
- Yarn needle

GAUGE

16 stitches by 20 rows = 4" in stockinette

continued ›››

INSTRUCTIONS

Cast on 90 (90, 94, 102, 106, 106, 110, 110) sts.

Row 1 (RS): K20 (20, 21, 23, 24, 24, 25, 24), pm, k8 (8, 8, 8, 8, 8, 8, 10), pm, k34 (34, 36, 40, 42, 42, 44, 42), pm, k8 (8, 8, 8, 8, 8, 8, 10), pm, k20 (20, 21, 23, 24, 24, 25, 24).

Row 2: K6, p to 6 sts from end, k6.

Row 3: [K to 1 st before next marker, m1r, k1, sm, k1, m1l] *four times*, k to end of row. [98 (98, 102, 110, 114, 114, 118, 118) stitches on needle at end of row]

Row 4: K6, p to 6 sts from end, k6.

Row 5: Repeat Row 3. [106 (106, 110, 118, 122, 122, 126, 126) sts on needle]

Row 6: K6, p to 6 sts from end, k2, bind off 2 sts, k2. [104 (104, 108, 116, 120, 120, 124, 124) sts on needle]

Row 7: K2, cast on 2 sts using short-tail cast-on method, [k to 1 st before next marker, m1r, k1, sm, k1, m1l] *four times*, k to end of row. [114 (114, 118, 126, 130, 130, 134, 134) sts on needle]

Row 8: K6, p to 6 sts from end, k6.

Rows 9–14: Repeat Rows 3 and 4, *three times*. [end with 138 (138, 142, 150, 154, 154, 158, 158) sts on needle]

Row 15: Repeat Row 3. [146 (146, 150, 158, 162, 162, 166, 166) sts on needle]

Row 16: Repeat Row 6. [144 (144, 148, 156, 160, 160, 164, 164) sts on needle]

Row 17: Repeat Row 7. [154 (154, 158, 166, 170, 170, 174, 174) sts on needle]

Row 18: K6, p to 6 sts from end, k6.

Rows 19–22: Repeat Rows 3 and 4, *two times*. [end with 170 (170, 174, 182, 186, 186, 190, 190) sts on needle]

JOINING IN THE ROUND

Place the 6 sts from the beginning of Row 22 onto a DPN. Bring the DPN behind the first 6 sts of Round 23.

Round 23: [K1 into next st and first available st of DPN as 1 st (see tutorial on page 52)] *six times*, [k to 1 st before next marker, m1r, k1, sm, k1, m1l] *four times*, k to end of round. [172 (172, 176, 184, 188, 188, 192, 192) sts on needle]

Round 24: P6, k to end of round.

Round 25: [K to 1 st before next marker, m1r, k1, sm, k1, m1l] *four times*, k to end of round. [180 (180, 184, 192, 196, 196, 200, 200) sts on needle]

Round 26: P6, k to end of round.

Round 27: [K to 1 st before next marker, m1r, k1, sm, k1, m1l] *four times*, k to end of round. [188 (188, 192, 200, 204, 204, 208, 208) sts on needle]

Round 28: K all sts.

Rounds 29, 30 (38, 44, 50, 56, 64, 70, 78): Repeat Rounds 27, 28. [end with 196 (228, 256, 288, 316, 348, 376, 408) sts on needle]

SIZE 36" ONLY

Round 31: [K to next marker, sm, k1, m1l, k to 1 st before next marker, m1r, k1, sm] *two times*, k to end of round. [200 sts on needle]

Round 32: K all sts.

Rounds 33–36: Repeat Rounds 31, 32. [end with 208 sts on needle]

SIZE 40" ONLY

Round 39: [K to next marker, sm, k1, m1l, K to 1 st before next marker, m1r, k1, sm] *two times*, k to end of round. [232 sts on needle]

Round 40: K all sts.

SIZES 36 (40, 44, 48, 52)" ONLY

Rounds 37 (41, 45, 51, 57)–48 (52, 56, 58, 62): K all sts.

continued > > >

ALL SIZES

Separation round: Removing markers as you go, K34 (38, 42, 46, 50, 54, 58, 62), place next 42 (46, 50, 58, 64, 72, 78, 86) sts on waste yarn, cast on 10 sts using short-tail cast-on method, k62 (70, 78, 86, 94, 102, 110, 118), place next 42 (46, 50, 58, 64, 72, 78, 86) sts on second waste yarn, cast on 10 sts using short-tail cast-on method, k to end of round. [144 (160, 176, 192, 208, 224, 240, 256) sts on needle]

BODY

Rounds 1–70: K all sts.

Rounds 71–80: [K2, p2] *to end of round.*

Bind off and weave in ends.

SLEEVES (MAKE 2)

Place live sts from one waste yarn onto DPNs. With the new yarn and working needle, pick up 10 sts evenly from 10 sts cast-on under the armhole. Place the marker between the 5th and 6th picked-up sts. [52 (56, 60, 68, 74, 82, 88, 96) sts on needle]

Rounds 1–5 (5, 5, 13, 7, 10, 5, 13): K all sts.

Round 6 (6, 6, 14, 8, 11, 6, 14): K to 2 sts before marker, ssk, sm, k2tog, k to end of round. [50 (54, 58, 66, 72, 80, 86, 94) sts on needle]

Rounds 7 (7, 7, 15, 9, 12, 7, 15)–13 (13, 13, 19, 13, 15, 10, 17): K all sts.

Rounds 14 (14, 14, 20, 14, 16, 11, 18)–85: Repeat Rounds 6 (6, 6, 14, 8, 11, 6, 14)–13 (13, 13, 19, 13, 15, 10, 17). [end with 32 (36, 40, 44, 48, 52, 56, 60) sts on needle]

Rounds 86–100: [K2, p2] *to end of round.*

Bind off and weave in ends.

COLLAR

Pick up and knit 78 (78, 82, 90, 94, 94, 98, 98) sts along neckline starting at 7th stitch of beginning cast-on of sweater and ending at 6 sts from end of cast-on.

Rows 1–18 (18, 18, 18, 22, 22, 22, 22): K all sts.

Bind off and weave in ends.

FINISHING

Block the garment to the finished measurements. Stitch on two buttons opposite the buttonholes using new yarn and a yarn needle.

MEASUREMENTS

Chest Circumference **A**: 36 (40, 44, 48, 52, 56, 60, 64)"/91.5 (101.5, 112, 122, 132, 142, 152.5, 162.5) cm

Body Length **B**: 16"/40.5 cm

Raglan Depth **C**: 9½ (10½, 11¼, 11½, 12½, 12¾, 14, 15½)"/24 (26.5, 28.5, 29, 32, 32.5, 35.5, 39) cm

Armhole Circumference **D**: 13 (14, 15, 17, 18½, 20½, 22, 24)"/33 (35.5, 38, 43, 47, 52, 56, 61) cm

Wrist Circumference **E**: 8 (9, 10, 11, 12, 13, 14, 15)"/20 (23, 25.5, 28, 30.5, 33, 35.5, 38) cm

Sleeve Length **F**: 20"/51 cm

Neck Circumference **G**: 21 (21, 22, 24, 25, 25, 26, 26)"/53 (53, 56, 61, 63.5, 63.5, 66, 66) cm

RESOURCES

SOURCES FOR MATERIALS:

Berroco Berroco.com
Clover Needlecraft Clover-USA.com
Knit Picks KnitPicks.com
LoveCrafts LoveCrafts.com

REFERENCE VIDEOS:

Arne & Carlos YouTube Channel YouTube.com/c/ARNECARLOS
Drowning in Yarn YouTube Channel YouTube.com/c/DrowninginYarn
Marly Bird YouTube Channel YouTube.com/@MarlyBird
VeryPink Knits YouTube Channel YouTube.com/user/verypinkknits

BOOKS FOR FURTHER STUDY:

Hiatt, June Hemmons. *The Principles of Knitting.* Simon & Schuster, 1988.
Stanley, Montse. *Reader's Digest Knitter's Handbook.* Reader's Digest, 1993.
Vogue Knitting: The Ultimate Knitting Book: Completely Revised and Updated. Sixth & Spring Books, 2018.
Vogue Knitting: The Ultimate Stitch Dictionary. Sixth & Spring Books, 2021.

INDEX

ACKNOWLEDGMENTS

This book would not have been possible without the help and guidance of many. I would like to share my most sincere gratitude to the following people and businesses: Shannon Roudhán and Jason Bowlsby, thank you for your invaluable advice and knowledge over the years. The team at Callisto Publishing, thank you for the countless hours spent working to enhance (and correct, I'm sure) my work for this project. A heartfelt thanks to Jen Joyce; without your recommendation, none of this would have happened. Thank you also to LoveCrafts, Berroco, Knit Picks, and Clover Needlecraft for supplying all the yarn and tools featured in this book. Finally, a special thank-you to my main support system—my mother, Melissa Stark; sister, Emery Stark; dear friend Olivia Moffet; and partner, Rayce Rockey. I love you all more than words can say.

ABOUT THE AUTHOR

QUAYLN STARK has established himself as a strong presence in the fiber arts scene, designing patterns for many companies within the field as well as one-of-a-kind garments for celebrities and influencers. Unique shaping and outlandish concepts help Stark push the boundaries of what it means to be a fiber arts designer in the social age. The mission statement of his design house, QUOE, has always been to "Break the Status," and as such, embraces everyone who isn't scared to step outside the established perimeters of crafting, art, and fashion.

When he is not freelance designing, Stark can usually be found at home working on personal design projects focusing on the artistic aspects of textile work while listening to an audiobook or podcast. Track the progress of his many yarn and fiber educed escapades on Instagram at @portquoelio and TikTok at @QUOE.

NOTES

NOTES

NOTES

NOTES

NOTES